Land of Trumpin

Land of Trumpin

Marc Munroe Dion

Creators Publishing
Hermosa Beach, CA

The Land of Trumpin
Copyright © 2017 Marc Munroe Dion

Cover art by Emely DelSanto
Creative Coordinator Peter Kaminski

CREATORS PUBLISHING
737 3rd St
Hermosa Beach, CA 90254
310-337-7003

Library of Congress Control Number: 2017937597
ISBN (print): 9781945630521
ISBN (ebook): 9781945630514

First Edition
Printed in the United States of America
1   3   5   7   9   10   8   6   4   2

To my wife, Deborah.

Two only children adrift in a darkening universe.

Contents

Foreword by Thomas Frank   1

Chapter One: I Saw It Coming   3

Chapter Two: Songs of Casual Hate   31

Chapter Three: Land of Trumpin   55

Chapter Four: Roll Over and Play Dead   71

Chapter Five: Side-of-the-Mouth Stories   91

Acknowledgements   126

About the Author   127

Foreword by Thomas Frank

The hard-boiled working-class style that used to be a staple of opinion journalism in this country is no longer in vogue. But when you read the columns of Marc Munroe Dion you start to realize how very much you miss it. You understand how wholesome it can be for our country and our common life.

In Dion's accounts of life in the crumbling mill town of Fall River, Massachusetts, this tough-minded, sarcastic sensibility makes a sort of last scoffing stand against the indifferent white-collar world.

Dion's derision is satisfying. It is healthful. He laughs at the follies of the political class. He cheers for the bravery of workers who, here and there, stand up to their bosses. And he carefully documents the slow disintegration of the American dream: a society where drug use is epidemic, where the toxic allure of Donald Trump seems unstoppable.

It is a hard, bitter story, but in Dion's pages it becomes a joy to read.

—Thomas Frank
Adapted from *Listen, Liberal* (Metropolitan Books, 2016)

Chapter One

I Saw It Coming

November 14, 2016

Waiting for the Leader

The middle and working classes in America are falling behind. Well, the middle class is falling behind. The working class tore up the card in the union they once belonged to and left the world.

And we're mad. We focus our rage on black people who receive welfare. In America, today, we talk about welfare recipients the way Hitler talked about Jews.

We are "cheated" out of victory in war after war because the enemy won't "fight fair." We believe we would have won in Vietnam if we'd just have bombed the place a little more.

We long for some mythical America when you could hit your kids as much as you wanted and call black people anything you wanted. Beating your kids makes them strong, like real Americans.

We love the flag and we orchestrate orgiastic flag displays in front of public buildings and at sporting events where many of the players either weren't born in this country or were born in the huge, festering ghettoes we maintain as NFL nurseries.

We hate college professors. They make the nation weak with whack-job theories about equality. We hate political correctness. "Why do we have to be so afraid of offending people," we whine in the tone of the deeply offended.

We want a brutally simple "common sense" approach to government. Term limits. Bombs. No having the "gay agenda crammed down our throats," whatever, shudder, that means.

We want a return to the real American ethos, to the

Puritan, to the cowboy, to the Bible and the pistol.

People who dislike anything we do are "crazy" and they practice a "religion of hate." Kill 'em and take their oil.

Our culture is vanishing under a wave of gabbling foreigners. They don't look like us, they don't smell like us, and they long to breed with our pale daughters. Sadly, some of our pale daughters have proven to be agreeable, as have some of our white-skinned sons.

We gotta do something. We gotta find the right man. The true leader. Someone who will, "cut through the red tape" and end the political correctness. That is the reason you don't have a job. We need someone who will pry the EBT cards out of thousands of greedy, grasping black hands, which will cause greater respect for the flag and bring prayer back to the schools. We want the Muslims rounded up and put somewhere, anywhere. That'll give your kid a better shot at running a 24-hour convenience store in a bad neighborhood.

Hey, in America, if you're smart and you work hard, you get rich, no? Well, you're not rich and you know you're not lazy or stupid, so someone, probably a welfare mother or a Muslim cab driver, has stolen your opportunity. Get a gun and take it back!

This road only goes one way. Practice saying, "Heil!"

✪✪✪

January 25, 2016

Resist Government Control?

I got two tickets last week. Same truck. Same time.

The first ticket was for parking on the sidewalk. There is a small noncurbed portion of sidewalk (not a wheelchair access) right in front of the newspaper where I work. I regard it as a parking space. The city does not. This is a philosophical dispute.

The second ticket was for having an expired inspection sticker on my truck. I hadn't noticed. This is not a dispute, nor does it involve any philosophy. At best, I can say that a bloated, out-of-control government has decided to impose arbitrary standards on my vehicle. If I fail to meet their arbitrary standards, they confiscate some of my hard-earned money.

The total for both tickets was $70. I considered my options.

I could have decided to vote for Donald Trump but, while I am white and middle-aged and I was angry, I'm not crazy and I do not admire the Third Reich. Besides, that solution did not promise immediate assistance.

I considered taking action of a far more drastic sort.

I figured I could go get a gun, and defend this little piece of my rights. I don't own a gun, and I don't have any kind of license or permit, but I haven't been a newspaper reporter for 30 years without knowing how to buy an illegal gun. I live in an economically depressed urban area. Out in the suburbs, you may think the government is coming to take your guns. Here in cracked-sidewalk America, we know nobody's running out of guns anytime soon.

Once I had the gun, I could walk six blocks to the army surplus store, grab a set of fatigues and pick up an American flag. Total cost? Maybe $30. I had that on me, and it's better to spend your money on a flag and some scraps of a uniform than it is to give it to the confiscatory government.

After I had the gun, the uniform scraps and the flag, all I had to do was "occupy" the piece of sidewalk/parking space on which my truck was sitting. I could say I was doing it to preserve all our freedoms, to make clear the will of the founders. I have some Native-American blood in me on my Pop's side so, if worse came to worse; I could always insist I was reclaiming my ancestral land.

I was pretty thrilled there for a minute. Two hundred bucks for a thirdhand pistol, $30 for the scraps of uniform and the flag, and I'd be a patriot, ready to die for this sacred piece of sidewalk/parking space.

I didn't do it, of course. I took the ticket off the windshield and, that night, I wrote a check for $70, and I put it in the envelope provided.

You know why?

Because I am one of the people who pay. We pay the taxes and the tickets. Your slogans may sound fierce and your bumper sticker may be threatening, but the ones who pay run the country.

✪✪✪

February 1, 2016

Dry Eye

I had to go buy a little bottle of artificial tears for my mother tonight. That's an odd thing to be buying in America right now — crying is very nearly forbidden.

She's 87. She has dry eye. The rest of us don't cry because it means we're weak and we have feelings for things. School shootings. The homeless. The poor. We argue over those things, and we use them to score points, but we do not cry.

I went to a dollar store on an urban street, across from a Chinese restaurant whose menu includes fried plantains, next to a Pakistani-run cigarette and convenience store, two doors down from an auto parts store.

When I got to the register at the dollar store with my $2.15 bottle of tears, there was an old-style school bell on the counter and a hand-lettered sign reading, "Ring bell for service."

I rang.

A woman in her 30s, short and round, came in from outside, where she'd been standing, smoking a cigarette.

"Sorry," she said.

"It's all right," I said. "You were on your break. I get breaks on my job."

"Especially when you've been here since 8," she said.

It was 7 p.m.

"I just got off," I told her. "I started at 9."

"I'm here till 10," she told me.

"You win," I said. "I'm working 11 days straight, though. You?"

"I'm off Sunday," she said.

8

"I win that one," I told her.

She laughed.

"We're even then," she said. "You want a little bag for that?"

"That's OK," I said.

I put the bottle of tears in my pocket and left the store.

I'm writing this and it's 8:30 p.m., so I guess we're both still working, but at least I'm doing it in my own home, in stocking feet, smoking a pipe. If I want to go to the bathroom, I don't have to put a little bell and a note on my desk.

It strikes me, in my cold little home office, next to an un-insulated wall, that those of us who work at anything should love each other, should care for each other and, yes, should cry for each other.

A million cruel voices tell me to look down on that woman, to climb up on my master's degree and look way down at her and she should have tried harder. Hundreds of angry political voices tell me the working poor are funny tattooed clowns who earn exactly what they're worth. See the slumped little man sweeping the floor in the bank? Dumb good-for-nothing. He oughta learn English if he's gonna come here.

And the funny thing is, the guys at the very top can't tell the difference between white-collar me and the guy sweeping the floor. They set us at each other's throats and they pay us the lowest wages they can. Suburb hates trailer park. Trailer park hates black ghetto. Everybody knows the guy one step further down the ladder deserves to be there because he's lazy.

We all have dry eye.

✪✪✪

February 8, 2016

Shot Below the Belt

A couple of people described glancingly in news stories as "top Army and Marine Corps generals" just told the Senate every military job will be open to women in the next few years. The White House, I guess, will still be tenanted by people who ran screaming from military service. This proves once again that the "new economy" gives poor people plenty of chances to better themselves and learn to kill people.

Women can join the military now, of course, and when they are through, they can return honorably to whatever minimum wage job they were trying to avoid in the first place. Yep. Your kids go to war. Their kids go to college.

Joining the military is a great way to get money for college. This is particularly true if your Desert Storm veteran dad came back from the war so crazy he couldn't hold a job, so you reach 18 without enough money to buy gum. Here's the gun! Off you go and pray you don't come back like Daddy!

It's an even better deal if you're a kid with two addicted parents and you're in the foster care system. Once you hit 18, you have to say goodbye to your foster parents. It's called "aging out of the system," and it is a great encourager of armed patriotism.

In the entire history of war, no nation has ever found a faster way to raise an army than grabbing the poor off the street. They're thankful for the food; their parents don't raise much fuss; and, if they don't come back, who's gonna miss another motel maid or dishwasher? It's not like you're decimating the next crop of investment bankers.

I have had my chain steakhouse meal served to me by a

part-time, no-benefits waiter with an open food stamp account who only months before had been earning the "Thank you for your service" we throw at vets like a drunk heaving a quarter tip at a bartender. What a lucky American I am to have so many cheap meals served to me by so many cheap "heroes" that you hardly have to pay at all. You took Mosul, now you're takin' my order.

And there are so many places to fight. Iran. Iraq. Lebanon. Syria. Ferguson, Missouri. They're going to need men. And women. Maybe some of those child soldiers they have in Africa. I know women who would sell their 10 year old to the army for $1,000. Who are we kidding? You can get a kid for a lot less than a grand. Try the heroin addict parents first. A lot of them have been in the military, so they know it's not a bad life. Not as bad as the projects, anyway.

I believe people who serve in the military should come back to a country where it is not just theoretically "possible" to rise from poverty. I think it should be likely you'll rise from poverty. It's what happened to my old man when he got back from World War II, and he wasn't even a little bit grateful. He just thought that's how America worked.

✪✪✪

February 22, 2016

A Confederate Solution

In Tennessee, where presumably everyone has a job and enough food to eat, the House of White People's Representatives just passed a law making it harder to remove statues of Confederate generals or rename streets named after Confederate heroes.

It's winter, and the poor people of Tennessee can have all the ice water they want. That simple statement reminds me of the Civil War, when boys we would think of as college-aged lay wounded on battlefields for days, crying for water. Then, they died.

The Civil War wasn't one of those inconclusive, Vietnam-type wars. It was over when it was over. The Confederacy gave up, surrendered, chucked in the towel, quit, couldn't take any more, went belly up and cried "uncle." They lost.

Southern states stayed in the Union. The slaves were freed.

The preservation of the Union came about because the Confederacy lost the war. They lost. They lost, and they didn't come back for a second try because they lost so convincingly.

There's that word again. Lost. The Confederacy lost the war. They surrendered.

And I'm happy about that because slavery was a horror and splitting the Union to save slavery or states' rights was a horrible idea.

The losers of that war didn't want to fight any more but they didn't want to give up a flag made meaningless by surrender, so they built statues of the guys on the losing side wherever they could. And that very southern town was soon

12

graced by a statue of General Whuppem T. Lynchrope, a justifiably famous man who lost, whose army surrendered, whose country ceased to exist but will not go away.

And what's left are the flags and the statues cast and carried by the side that lost, and the grubby little grabbing for votes that still animates the self-proclaimed descendants of those men who lost the war.

It's a dirty little game, dishonoring the noble dead by pretending to fight a war they themselves quit. Say what you want about the noble warriors of the South's Lost Cause, they knew when they'd had enough, when flesh would bear no more, when to end the fighting and the dying and the starving.

The hands of the men who really fought the war took the flag down at the end, surrendered their guns, gave it up and went home to whatever was left at home. They wanted it to be over so much that they surrendered. They had to be sure the other side knew they were done. The stories got made up later, when no one was afraid of dying anymore.

I say leave the statues of the Confederate generals right where they've always been, as a way to remember the honored dead and those who quit in the end. And next to each Confederate statue, erect a statue of Dr. Martin Luther King Jr. as a way to remember the honored dead and those who never quit.

February 29, 2016

Trump Supporters, 'You'll Be Sorry!'

I had a friend who worked as a guard in a state prison.

"It's amazing how these guys think," he told me one morning, when we were both off work and drinking coffee in a diner across the street from an abandoned paper box factory.

"The prisoners," he said. "They don't think like we do. Everything is somebody else's fault."

I kept drinking coffee and let him tell his story.

"The other day, they're lined up to get their meds," he said. "You can't let 'em keep their own pills 'cause they'd crush 'em up and snort 'em or sell 'em or take 'em all at once.

"And one of the guys, he's in line to get his meds and he doesn't have a shirt on.

"So I tell him, 'You can't be in line without a shirt. You gotta go back to your cell and get your shirt and put it on.'

"Guy starts raisin' all kinds of hell with me," my friend said, as the waitress gave him a refill on his coffee. "He's tellin' me it's hot and he doesn't wanna wear a shirt and he doesn't wanna go all the way back to his cell and it's not a fair rule.

"I tell him there's nothing I can do about it; it's just the rule, and, if he wants his meds, he's gonna have to go back to his cell and get his shirt."

My prison guard buddy started laughing.

"So, the guy looks at me and he says, 'Well, then I'm just not going to take my meds!'"

"Like I'm his mother or somethin'," my friend said to me. "What do I care if he takes his meds? What am I gonna do, be sad if he dies?"

"But that's how they think," he said. "Nothing's their fault. They shoot dope and they molest kids and they rob old

14

ladies and they get arrested and locked up and it's just everybody picking on 'em. And they think that if they don't take their meds and they die, that's gonna be somebody else's fault, too. They just wanna destroy everybody else and themselves 'cause things ain't goin' their way."

I paid for my friend's breakfast. As I remember, it was $5.75 for two pancakes, sausage and coffee. I paid because I knew I'd use his story someday. Just because you pick a story up in the street doesn't mean you shouldn't at least look around for somebody to pay.

I watch the disappointed, angry voters line up for Donald Trump, line up in a country with stagnant middle- and working-class incomes, watch them line up in a country where people with a high school diploma can't find a union job, watch them line up in a country where, election after election, we vote in people who let us keep our guns and our God while they take everything else.

And I hear voices saying, "I'm not gonna take my meds. I'm gonna vote for Trump. I'll do it. I really will. You'll be sorry."

March 7, 2016

Who Cares What I Think About Donald Trump?

Because not enough reporters, columnists and editors asked themselves that question, the country is now being blackjacked by a Donald Trump candidacy that will change America, whether he wins or loses.

In most newsrooms, the first announcement of a Trump candidacy led to jokes about comb-overs and casinos.

And there it lay, while the news people, used to the incumbents and the expected candidates, went back to the safe little press conferences and the pre-chewed press releases, while around us rose a howl of discontent that could not be heard through the brick walls of the newspaper building, could not penetrate the soundproof safety of the broadcast studio.

We missed the story. We walked right past every blaze of middle and working class anger that heated up the Trump campaign. We couldn't even smell the smoke. House fires we could cover, but we missed the flames that engulfed a nation.

We blew it. Trump talked to crowds of people who are afraid they'll lose their guns, afraid there will be Sharia in Alabama, angry because the plant closed but the welfare people kept their checks.

Read the "think pieces" newspapers have done about Trump in the last few months. How many of those articles explained patiently why Trump was going to lose or why he should lose? The articles are wishes, desperate notes to God begging him to strike down Donald Trump.

I've been a full-time newspaper employee for 33 years,

more than half my life, and I have never been as ashamed of my business as I am right now.

We decided Trump had no chance. We decided Trump would fade after the first primary. We decided his supporters were too dimwitted to count.

If America's mainstream media could have abandoned its anti-working class bigotry for a second, we would have taken Trump seriously from the first day. We would have ripped into his finances, his personal life and his associations. We would not have done a hatchet job on him, but would have found out who he was and how he worked and what he wanted. We would have done our job on its most basic level.

Instead, we told the jokes and we relentlessly ignored the people we regard as fat-bellied NASCAR fans who buy the paper but are secretly despised by the people who write what's in the paper.

By the time we remembered that people we look down on could vote it was too damn late. We hadn't done our jobs.

We're reporters. We can duck under the crime scene tape. We can get the senator on the phone. We stand in the front, but we come and go through the back door, avoiding the crowd. We joke with the incumbents, little private jokes. We know who is going to get the nomination. We know who is going to win.

This time we were wrong, and we were wrong because we failed to ask ourselves, "Who cares what I think about Donald Trump? What do other people think?"

❂❂❂

March 14, 2016

You Mean It If You Say It

Many years ago, in a newsroom where I toiled, there was an old crime reporter who would sometimes return to the office with the horrific details of domestic abuse.

"But he loves her," he would say after he told the story to the reporters.

"You know how she knows he loves her?" he would ask. "Because he told her he loves her."

It was a brutal, unkind thing to say, but he knew it was true and, as I journeyed further into the dark woods of life on a newspaper night shift, I began to say the same thing myself.

You know how you know a politician is a Christian?

Because he tells you he's a Christian.

He is a Christian when he says he is or when she says she is. And Christians they remain when they send your kid off to get killed in East Carbombistan, a country that, like America, is filled with true believers.

And I can guarantee you that, when your child's slightly mismatched body parts get stuffed into a box and flown home, the Christian politician will demand that your son or daughter's lifeless corpse receives a Christian burial.

When you are raising your orphaned grandchildren, the Christian politician will fight to the death to make sure they are allowed to include "Under God" in the Pledge of Allegiance at the beginning of classes in their underfunded ghetto grade school. The Christian politician does not give a damn if you and your orphaned grandchildren get enough to eat. In fact, the Christian politician is endeavoring to cut the food stamp program because he believes its main beneficiaries are black layabouts who reproduce every three months and drive new Mercedes convertibles.

You have no right to health insurance. You have no right to an education. You have no right to unionize. You have no right not to be called crude racial names. You have no right to sufficient food. You have no right to sleep indoors. You have no right to an abortion. You have no right to marry a member of your own sex.

You have the right to Jesus. Over and over again. You have the right to a full plate of Jesus three times a day. You have the right to a roof of Jesus over your head. You have the right to pray for the return of any and all things taken away from you or withheld from you by the Christian politician. You have the right to read the Bible, on the bus, while on the way to your nonunion, minimum wage, no-benefits, night shift second job. If the bus driver tells you to stop reading the Bible, the Christian politician will show up for a rally and will introduce legislation aimed at protecting the right of overworked, miserably poor people to read the Bible on city buses.

The domestic abuser hits you and claims to love you. The Christian politician hits you and claims to love Jesus.

✪✪✪

March 28, 2016

I'm Selling Out First Chance I Get

If America veers a little toward the stiff-armed-salute end of things, I'm selling out first chance I get.

I'm a 58-year-old white guy with seven years to go until retirement. However, I'd be willing to stay around longer if there was, say, a Ministry of Propaganda that needed professional writers to "explain" the new America and extol the Glorious Leader.

It won't be a private sector job, either. I've had those jobs all my life and what I've got to show for them is bad eyesight and a worse attitude.

The Ministry of Propaganda is going to be well-funded and loaded with pension jobs that come with private offices.

I'll be the guy who writes The Glorious Leader's biography. Donald Trump's never been in the military, you say? In my biography, he'll have been wounded during the firefight that killed Osama bin Laden.

I'll be the guy who explains that the new laws aren't really "segregation." They're laws defending small businesses from having to serve people they don't like. They're laws guaranteeing the right to private property that our Founding Fathers loved so much.

I'll explain why every war is self-defense. I'll explain why prohibiting any religion other than Christianity isn't bigotry; it's a "return to the Bible-based values on which this country was built." I'll explain the heroism of all military service and the sacredness of the flag.

I'll get a uniform. I know I will because the Ministry of Propaganda is a fighting unit dedicated to fighting our left-wing enemies here at home. Black is a nice uniform color.

Black is powerful. Don't worry, though. I won't be close to any shooting. Ministry of Propaganda lives are too precious to waste.

If there's any kind of rationing, you know us Ministry of Propaganda guys are going to get first dibs on the tobacco and whiskey. We'll need to smoke and drink a lot if we're going to successfully explain why rationing will guarantee total victory over our enemies.

I will never write the phrase "labor camp." They are "contained communities designed for the protection of their inhabitants."

My clever (and wholly paid-for) pen will explain why our defeats are actually victories and our massacres never happened.

Once the mass deportations start, there will be another perk to my job.

Let's say you're a woman, say 20 years old. (And trust me, some of us ministry guys are gonna like 'em a LOT younger.) Let's say you don't want to go back to Guatemala. I know people. I can help you. Have a cigarette. Have a drink. Relax.

I won't get in trouble for that, either. The New America will break the stranglehold of political correctness.

It's going to be a glorious world when America is great again. There will be jobs again, jobs for all kinds of people. All of it will be explained to you by cynical old hacks like me. Just remember: He who sells out first gets the best price.

✪✪✪

April 4, 2016

Sticking Your Finger in the Boss' Eye

I knew a guy once, a part-time politician, who held a series of elected offices on the city level. When he wasn't steering a very small ship of state, he worked at the county jail. He was the property room guy, in charge of cataloguing the belongings of arriving inmates, and returning them when time was served. It was an easy job, and he did it for a number of decades. He was a pudgy, gray-haired man with a chin shaped like the narrow end of an Anjou pear.

The sheriff was a large, red-faced man whose hair always looked freshly cut, and whose large gold badge hung always from the breast pocket of his dark suit. He won re-election every six years by taking things away from the prisoners. He ended smoking in the jail before that was common, and took television sets and radios way from the inmates.

"Jail shouldn't be a country club," he bellowed. Since all law-abiding, sensible, terrified middle-class people believe jail is exactly like a country club, he was landslided back into office.

Unbeknownst to the sheriff, his property room guy hated him very much, principally because the sheriff treated the jail employees' union as something else to be taken away.

When the small-time politician retired from the jail, he waited until he received his first pension check. Then, he announced he would quit his municipal office and run for sheriff. He knew he wouldn't win, since he was unknown outside of the municipality where he lived, but he had hatred and a secure pension check, and that was enough.

It was a fun campaign to cover. The challenger knew

things about the inner workings of the sheriff's department, and he'd picked up a great amount of guards' gossip. He used it all, barnstorming happily about the county, embarrassing the sheriff with the indelicate details of county government. The incumbent sheriff spent a lot of time pouring denial into my notebook.

The incumbent sheriff won re-election after he announced that chained gangs of inmates would begin picking up trash on county roads.

It occurs to me, as the national election jumps from horror to horror the way a monkey jumps from tree to tree, that perhaps all Donald Trump every really meant to do was run.

Trump is a businessman and, while business people pitchfork money at politicians, they don't like politicians. This is because the politician can make people listen and the businessperson cannot.

Maybe all Trump wanted was get a solid 10 percent of the vote and stick his thumb in the eyes of the real professionals.

Now he's stuck with it, watching in terror as he climbs in the polls, winning primaries, getting always closer to the job he doesn't want. His public utterances grow more boorish and threatening every week as he desperately attempts to drive his followers away, but it just won't work. Their appetite for debasement is bottomless.

Poor Donald Trump. If he's not careful, he's gonna win this thing.

✪✪✪

April 11, 2016

Candidates Walk Into a Bar

As someone who tended bar for a while back in graduate school, I not only believe alcohol reveals character, I believe drinking alcohol in public reveals character publicly.

So, as I contemplate the cast of characters running for president, I wonder what they might be like as bar patrons.

Donald Trump. Drinks top-shelf liquor. Tips well, but you have to listen to him tell you about how good his business is doing, how rich he is, how hot his wife is, how well he plays golf and how he got the better of everyone who ever tried to "screw" him.

Bernie Sanders. Cheap draft beer. Never buys a round. Asks you if you're in a union. Complains about the prices. Eats three bowls of the free popcorn. No tip. Tries to bond with construction workers at the bar, but they ignore him.

Hillary Clinton. White wine. Average tip. After three drinks, she cries and tells you about her husband's infidelities. After four, will go home with anyone.

Carly Fiorina. Light beer. Decent tip. Says nothing. Leaves alone. No one notices.

John Kasich. Comes in. Has one beer. Leaves without telling anyone. Comes back. Has another beer. Tips with change, but it adds up to a couple bucks.

Jeb Bush. Good bourbon. Hits on the prettiest girl in the place. Gets shot down. Calls his dad for a ride home. He doesn't tip, but when his dad shows up, he gives you $5 for taking care of his son.

Marco Rubio. After one martini, he tells you his immigrant father was a bartender. After two martinis, he tells you his immigrant father was a bartender. After three martinis, he tells you his immigrant father was a bartender. You don't care what he tips. You just want him to stop talking.

Ted Cruz. Tells you his evangelical faith is opposed to alcohol. Drinks straight tequila. Makes a grab for the waitress. No tip because you throw him out. Beaten badly in the parking lot by the waitress' boyfriend.

At the end of the night, you count your tip money. The $100 bill Trump gave you really made the night for you. Still, you hope he doesn't come back.

Five minutes till closing, Barack Obama walks in, sits at the bar, lights a cigarette. Plays "Stormy Monday" on the jukebox.

"Have I got time for one, Chief?" he asks you.

"Yeah," you say.

You pour him one and one for yourself.

"You know," you say. "It might be time for me to find something else. This place is much weirder than it was when I started and that's not even 10 years ago."

"Tell me about it," he says.

✪✪✪

April 18, 2016

Fear the Mob

You couldn't use the phrase today, but back a couple hundred years or so, people of learning and property feared what they called "the mob."

The mob was "we the people" at our worst, rampaging through the streets, burning the property of honest people, killing soldiers and what passed for police in those days, storming the king's palace. The mob could be blown by any wind, stirred to violence by any rumor, inflamed by blind prejudice, made love to by any orator who would pimp its lowest prejudices.

The mob is childish, but not at all cute. We do not call it a "lynch gathering," after all.

There are other reasons why the Electoral College exists in the United States, but one of the reasons it exists is as a buffer between the will of the public and the two highest offices in the land.

The Founding Fathers, wily compromisers all, feared royalty, religion and the mob.

Royalty they feared because it took the property of honest men. Religion they feared because people in Europe had been butchering each other for centuries over religion. The mob they feared because, while they didn't think people were stupid, they thought people did stupid things when they were frightened or excited or mad.

That they created the Electoral College proves their brilliance because only brilliant minds could identify and move subtly against such an ugly fact. The mob killed the czar and the king of France. Napoleon and Stalin restored order brutally. Riots in the streets birthed the Nixon presidency.

The mob, which is only normal people angry beyond reason, can burn and kill, can tear down and trample. It cannot rebuild or organize trash collection or make neighborhoods safe. After the mob goes its howling, torch-lit way, some strong man comes along; someone not afraid to use the whip. There follows a generation or two of repression, and a great deal of death. The trains run on time, but your husband is taken to a labor camp and starves to death.

Now, when the socialists are afraid they won't get Bernie Sanders and the fascists are afraid they won't get Donald Trump, we hear cries about how "stupid" and "unfair" the system is, something I've also heard at Little League games in regards to the umpire. The umpire is at the game to serve as a buffer between the mob in the stands and the final score. Without the umpire, you might as well declare a winner based on which team's fans make the most noise.

"Kill the umpire," used to be the stereotypical cry of the disappointed baseball fan. You can indeed kill the umpire, but it doesn't lead to a better game.

God bless the Founding Fathers. They didn't trust us at all.

✪✪✪

April 25, 2016

An Exciting New Opportunity for My Readers

In your emails to me, many of you have mentioned that I don't write enough columns reflecting your opinions about guns, Jesus, political correctness, the Federal Reserve Bank, Mexicans, Muslims, spanking, gay marriage, bathroom rights and privileges, abortion, the Book of Revelations and the fact that black slavery "wasn't so bad."

That's why I'm announcing my new "Personalized Column Program," an exciting, brutally capitalist plan that allows you to see your crazy opinions in print.

Here's how it works.

In the coming weeks, you will receive an emailed copy of my "personalized column form." The form, which was created without the use of blood-sucking, lazy union labor, will be emailed to you from, and was created in, a sweleringly oppressive Third World country where workers who did not produce their daily quota of emails were beaten to death.

When you receive the form, fill it out carefully, including your name, address, gender and religious affiliation. There are only two genders two chose from—male and female—and I will throw away any form sent to me by non-Christians. Whaddaya think I'm running here, some kind of gay pagan business?

On page two of the form, you will find a spacious and comfortable box in which to write just what you would like me to say in your personalized column.

If you cannot fit your request in the box provided,

please feel free to attach additional pages, on which you may write in your own blood as proof of sincerity.

Permitted language includes vile personal attacks on nonwhites and non-Christians, demeaning statements about women and the poor and impassioned pleas against vaccination, fluoridation and mongrelization of the white race.

Please include all relevant documentation, including pages torn from the Bible, "secret" Masonic documents, copies of President Obama's Kenyan birth certificate and a 400-page transcript of your correspondence with the Mudwallow County police department concerning their unlawful confiscation of your guns after you pistol-whipped your wife nearly to death.

When you have completed the form (and it's probably going to take a few months) send it to me along with $475,000 in cash. I cannot accept online payments at this time, but I hope to offer that option after I move to a small Caribbean nation.

Your personalized column purchase is important to me, and your column will be written in the order it was received. You can expect to see your opinion in print as soon as I go "off the grid" and get to some remote beach where the lying liberal government can't keep me from writing the truth. Be patient.

Complete confidentiality is guaranteed. Your personalized column will appear under my name, so if you have any warrants out, no one is going to come looking for you. Only you and the members of your white supremacist brotherhood will ever have to know it's actually YOUR opinion.

Freedom of the press isn't free. You have to pay me.

✪✪✪

Chapter Two

Songs of Casual Hate

May 2, 2016

Serbia Elects the American President

In Mladenovac, Serbia, a town not unlike Steubenville, Ohio, Luka Maksimovic and some of his bros started making videos poking fun at politicians. They're all in their 20s, young guys with a video camera and probably a case or two of beer.

They invented Serbian politician Ljubisa Beli, a political fool who made his video appearances bare-chested on a white horse.

Beli was crude and dishonest, owned a shady business and loudly announced he had no intention of playing by the rules. He promised jobs everyone knew he couldn't deliver. He even promised to make restaurants serve better sandwiches. He handed out forged college degrees to his supporters. I imagine he was a great hit with waiters and customers, two groups that include nearly everyone.

Mladenovac, where this all happened, is a decaying manufacturing town full of closed factories and people who feel like they've been hit from behind with a tire tool.

They can take a joke in Mladenovac. They have to because the jokes are all they have left. I live in a town like that in Massachusetts. I have a friend who does a dead-on impersonation of a junkie, high, bending slowly forward from the waist until his head touches his feet. Around here, we call that "the dope fiend lean." My friend's impersonation is hilarious, extremely cruel and very sad.

The Serb-bros must have had big fun in mom's basement, making the video, laughing, not caring how many cigarettes they smoked because they're still too young to wheeze.

The Balkan bros also ran for office and they won seats

on the local version of an American city council. Fictitious character Beli also won, but he will not serve. One of the differences between American politics and Serbian politics is that fictional characters cannot hold office in Serbia. If America had that rule, Ronald Reagan would have died in the Second-Rate Old Actors Home.

The bros promise reform, and they promise to take it all seriously. One of the hardest parts of growing up is learning to take things seriously. Eventually, you get old enough to take everything seriously, which is the beginning of death.

In America, our Donald Trump is everything the fictional sleaze Beli is, except Trump is real, or at least he claims he's real. Trump has even handed out the fake diplomas.

The factory jobs are gone from America, too, though Trump says he'll bring 'em back, presumably by going to China and telling them to give us back the jobs. If they won't give the jobs back, he'll bomb hell out of 'em and take their women.

When the times were good in Mladenovac, nobody would have paid any attention to the videos made by a bunch of young guys all strung out on lack of respect and general goofiness. Instead, the citizens would have quietly elected some guy with an unmatched record of getting the garbage picked up and the snow plowed.

Some jokes don't translate well. The Mladenovac joke does. It translates to Trump, who is fictional enough to laugh at, but real enough to elect.

May 9, 2016

Trump-Arpaio—You're Doomed, You Liberal Sissy!

As Donald Trump jibbers and mugs atop a pile of sissy liberal skulls, the search is on for a running mate. One thing's certain, you're gonna need a cartoon character to match Trump.

Three words.

"America's Toughest Sheriff."

That's right, the perfect mate for Trump is the angry pencil sketch serving as sheriff of Maricopa County, Arizona, where Joe Arpaio's made prisoners wear pink underwear and live in sweltering tent cities, all the while being investigated for everything from racial profiling to failing to investigate sex crimes.

His elections are dirty; he hates women; he's cost his county millions in legal expenses, settlements and court awards; and he is well-loved for being exactly the kind of tough guy dumbass we like these days, when we hate teachers and love prison guards.

A lot of county sheriffs are idiots. It's a small job, and all you really have to do is run a jail. Since the jail is full of poor people, no one much cares how you run it, either.

If you think an idiot sheriff isn't ready for the national stage, take a look at Trump.

If white people who didn't go to college could walk out of high school and into a unionized factory job, like they did a few decades ago, Trump couldn't get elected to the Parks and Recreation Commission in Lonesome Pony, Alabama.

But they can't, so he can.

And Arpaio, all tough guy bluster and not a damn bit of results, is the perfect sidekick for a superhero candidate who climbed the tower of working-class rage and stands there, hitching at his utility belt and eyeing up the girlies on the streets of Gotham City.

If I understand working-class rage, I also understand its tragic misuse. Working-class rage is like that pistol you buy because it's your constitutional right and because, sooner or later, black men are going to break into our house and try to rape your wife.

Oh, sure, eventually you'll lose your job at the auto parts store and you'll get loaded on bargain price beer and you'll shoot yourself because the bank is going to take your house, but that doesn't count. You bought the gun to protect your house because it was all you could do with a bunch of liberals running the country.

Arpaio's perfect. He talks like a cheaply made western, is singular in his lack of accomplishment and doesn't take any guff from his prisoners, all of whom are poor people in chains.

He doesn't coddle prisoners. His jail isn't a country club. He served in the military, and he wears a gun every day. He can be worshipped as a veteran, as a cop and as a tough guy. In 2016 America, what else counts?

He'll put a boot in your ass. He'll kick your ass. He'll kick ass and take names. He'll get your ass on a chain gang and put your ass to work. He'll send your illegal ass back to Mexico. He will remain focused on your ass until America is great again.

Trump/Arpaio—they'll kick ass.

✪✪✪

May 30, 2016

Trump Exactly Backwards

When I'm not writing these columns, I'm a newspaper reporter. Today, I went out on what newspaper people call a "feature." The pastor of a Catholic church not too far from my office is going to celebrate a Latin Mass at his church this week.

I'm 59. I was one of the last kids to be trained to serve the Mass in Latin. "Serve" means help the priest. I wore a black robe and, over it, a snow white sort of smock. I had to memorize the altar boys' responses in Latin, though there were laminated "cheat cards" on the altar for kids with bad memories. I liked the Latin. It was the first consciously beautiful language I'd ever heard. If I'm a writer today, at least part of it is due to the sound of the old Latin Mass.

In the old days, the priest faced away from his flock. After they did away with the Latin Mass, priests began to celebrate Mass facing the people in the pews. The priest I spoke to today is a traditionalist.

"They said the priest had his back to the people," he said of the Mass as I knew it. "But that isn't true. He didn't have his back to them. He was facing God."

Most often, if you don't understand something, you're just looking at it the wrong way. Move a little to one side or the other, stand on your head or go around behind the thing and you'll understand.

I came out of the church and, while I reject the idea that I was inspired by God, I started thinking about Donald Trump.

And I got behind him.

I am supposed to be afraid of Donald Trump. Many

commentators are, if only because we didn't take him seriously from the start and that embarrasses us. Because of this, we compare him to Hitler, because everyone knows that Hitler was the only Nazi in Germany.

And that isn't true. Hitler was popular. He was the people's choice. He was the savior. He said what other people were thinking. He spoke his mind.

Behind him there was a huge mass of Germans, beaten down by a lost war, beaten up by a depression, jobless, sure they were being cheated and manipulated by the Jews.

And behind Trump there is a huge mass of Americans, beaten down by purposeless wars they never win, beaten up by the loss of unionized factory work, jobless, sure they are losing their Jesus to the gays and their hard-earned money to crack-smoking welfare blacks.

They are my people. I come from a working-class family. When I was a kid, my father was a bartender and my mother was a clerk in a bank. I've worked on loading docks and in laundries. I've worked in furniture warehouses and as a security guard. In those jobs, I learned to love my own struggling, humorous, stubborn, dead-too-soon people.

I'm 59, the altar boy grown old, and God is far away and I'm afraid of my own kind.

June 6, 2016

The Long Weekend

You don't hear much about it anymore, but I keep thinking about Donald Trump's wall on the border with Mexico. I guess that's still something we might do here in the land of the free.

If you think we've got Mexicans in the country illegally NOW, just wait until 10,000 wall-building jobs show up on the Mexican border. You're not gonna be able to keep Carlos and the boys from swimming the river, not if there are construction jobs on the other side. And, once they run out of American laborers who can pass the drug test, contractors are going to start hiring (and underpaying) our docile little Mexican brothers.

I spent much of the recent Memorial Day weekend notebook deep in a reporter's celebration. That means I made overtime for covering three memorial services and a parade. I saw white doves released on three different occasions.

The memorials get bigger and the ceremonies get longer the more wars America fails to win, yet doesn't exactly lose. In addition, every ceremony does some heavy harkening back to World War II, the last war we won outright. If America fights four more draws, I predict Memorial Day will last until Christmas.

Once we get the wall built, we can't just walk away from it and expect the dang thing to keep the Mexicans out. They'll show up at night with ladders. They'll lasso the towers and pull themselves over. They'll get tangled in the barbed wire on top, but sooner or later, they'll be working in a Chicago car wash.

You're going to need guards on the wall, and not the

Border Patrol, either. There are not enough Border Patrol agents to stand shoulder-to-shoulder on top of the wall, three shifts a day, seven days a week. Anyway, they make too much money. It'd cost us a fortune to keep the wall manned.

You're going to need an army for that, and we've got an army. We've got an Army Reserve, too. We've got a National Guard. They've all been to Iraq and Afghanistan, too, so they're used to the kind of desert conditions you find down on the border.

And it's not like the soldiers can stand on the wall with bullhorns and shout at the Mexicans, "Hey, we've got an army up here. You better go home!"

When they had a wall to keep people from escaping East Germany, the soldiers on top would shoot you dead if you so much as touched the wall. It's the only thing that works. So, someday, if we build the wall, your son or daughter who joins the Army will be rotated to the border with his her unit and told to do wall duty.

And he or she will sit, with a rifle, and shoot the Mexicans who make a run at the wall. Men. Women. Children. Young girls with babies in their arms.

Because that's how you do it. That's how you make a wall work.

June 20, 2016

Let's Talk About Science

I like to read about science, mostly because I don't understand it very well. I'm at home in a history book. I'm never uncomfortable with a novel. Science, though, well, science takes some effort. Maybe that extra effort is what I like.

So, I was pretty damn entranced when scientists figured out that violence is common in space. Seems humans now have better "hearing aids" to drop in on what's happening trillions of light-years away. Like the security camera outside an all-night mini-mart, the new equipment captures a lot of conflict.

Out in space, all kinds of things crash into each other. Black holes. Planets. Big masses of energy.

All sorts of mangling takes places as a result of this conflict, and scientists using the high-tech "hearing aids" can hear the violence of the universe. It comes through as kind of a "chirp," usually just one note, but sometimes two. It goes on all the time, too, not just on long weekends or when the weather gets hot.

The second time the scientists heard one of these post-violence chirps was on Christmas night last year. They believe these huge, violent collisions don't happen very often, but anyone who has worked as a reporter on a daily paper can tell you that Christmas is not a silent night.

It changes the way you think about the stars, which always look like bright little lives to me. Now, I have to think of the terrible violence happening just inches from their shining heads. Worse yet, any cries they might make won't be picked up by scientists for centuries in our time. By the time we hear it, it will be too late.

I've never owned a telescope. In fact, I think looking at the stars more closely might ruin them for me. Sometimes, after working a newspaper night shift, I stop on the path that leads to my front door and look up at the stars, which are always clearer and purer than the press conference or street-corner shooting I've covered that night.

Now, when I look up, I just picture the stars ducking and dodging, frightened and trying to flee their orbits as some huge, violent collision bears down on them from the deepest reaches of endless, dark space.

It's not a pleasant thought, though I'm sure it won't stop me from working, getting my truck inspected, eating candy bars and mowing my lawn. Whatever terrible thing is going on out of my sight doesn't touch me, not really, and I can always look down at the ground when I'm out at night. Nothing is safer than looking down at the ground.

I wrote this three days after hearing that a group of stars stopped shining in Orlando, Florida. For three days, I've watched America walk around with its eyes on the dirt because it's safer than looking up at the stars.

✪✪✪

June 27, 2016

Mental Illness and Policy

I did my mother's grocery shopping last Saturday. She's 88 years old and uses a walker, so most "outside" jobs are mine now. Heading home after I put the groceries way, I thought I'd stop for ice cream.

I parked in front of a corner store with a sign in the window reading, "Cigarettes Sold At Legal Minimum," went in and selected a chocolate-covered ice cream bar from the freezer. I went over to the counter to pay, holding the ice cream bar in my right hand and two $1 bills in my left hand.

"Any kind you want," said the guy in front of me at the counter.

"This kind?" said the heavy set Indian man behind the counter, holding up a blue pack of cigarettes.

"Any kind," the man in front of me said. "My name is Mikey, and I don't give a fuck."

There's a high-rise apartment building across from the store. Red brick and very tall, it houses elderly people, some drug addicts and a number of people whose problems are more difficult to define. Mikey had a jittery look in his eyes that is not uncommon in the neighborhood.

The clerk handed over the cigarettes and Mikey handed over some money. We were the only three people in the store.

"The devil is after me," Mike said.

The store owner silently handed over the change.

"And if some Hare Krishna kills me, you see what happens," Mikey said.

The guy behind the counter said nothing.

Mikey left, mumbling. I put my ice cream bar down on a mat decorated with words in praise of chewing tobacco.

42

"Lots of crazy people in this city," the store owner said, taking my money.

When the government builds housing for people who are being chased by the devil, they do not build it in the suburbs. People in the cities are told this is because we have the "services" needed by those who are one step ahead of Satan. People in the suburbs require no explanation.

"I learn one thing," the store owner said to me. "If you don't talk to them, they talk anyway, but if you talk to them, they talk more.

"I don't talk to them," he said.

He gave me my change.

"Come back again," he said.

"I will," I said.

I got in my truck, unwrapped the ice cream and ate it on the short drive home.

About two blocks from the store, I caught up with Mikey. He was walking down the sidewalk, screaming. Every so often, he stopped, took a clear plastic bottle from his pocket and poured a clear fluid onto the sidewalk. Maybe it was holy water. Other than members of the clergy, the Mikeys of the world are the people most likely to be carrying holy water.

I drove slowly when I drove past Mikey. People screaming on the sidewalk are more likely to run out into traffic than almost any other group of people

It was a Saturday. The societal safety net relaxes on Saturday. There's a good chance that the store owner provided the only "services" Mikey got that Saturday.

Unless he went to a gun store.

✪✪✪

July 4, 2016

Waaaah! The Gays Stole My America!

As gay people continue to force their thick, muscular agenda down my unwilling throat, I gag on the America we're losing so fast.

Fortunately, some people are fighting back.

I'm writing this on Heterosexual Pride Day, an internet piece of idiocy I wasn't sure how to celebrate. I didn't even have the day off.

When I did get off work, I drove over to my mother's house and spent a couple of hours with her. She's in her 80s and I'm an only child, so I do this every day. Then I went home to my wife. She's a girl. Gay marriage is permitted, but it is not compulsory.

I was unsatisfied.

See, the gay people get EVERYTHING these days. They're taking away my America.

Used to be only heterosexual couples could get married, but gay people took that away from us. Used to be, only girl and boy couples could go to prom, but gay people are taking that away, too.

Once upon a time, there were no gay characters on television shows. But the gays took that, too. You can't call 'em anything you want, either, not anymore. They took the very words out of our mouths and replaced them with their surprisingly long homosexual agenda.

But they really hurt us in the parades. They have whole gay parades now — two, three miles of gays forcing their gay agenda down your tender main street. You hold a Veteran's Day Parade, and the gay Marine Corps Vets force themselves right into the middle of the thing. You have a St. Patrick's Day

Parade, and the gay Irish people want to march with you. They serve in the Army; they run for office; they get married. Anything that is forbidden to them, they want.

Radical Muslims hate us for being Americans and Christians, but they hate gays for being American, Christian AND gay. Right there, the gay people get one more hate than we do.

We didn't have a Heterosexual Pride Day Parade in my city this year, so I couldn't go. Unfortunately, I'm still gargling with the homosexual agenda.

I like the idea, though. Gays have Gay Pride Day, so we have to have Heterosexual Pride Day. We won't take back America until we have everything they have.

So, last Wednesday night, I hired three guys off the street to call me a "hetero" and beat the hell out of me, because that's another thing gays get more of than I do.

It hurt, but having my jaw wired shut means I can't open my mouth wide enough to get the homosexual agenda shoved down my throat.

✪✪✪

July 25, 2016

No Lives Matter

I think this may be when black and white in America finally have it out, when we finish the race war that began at the end of the Civil War. There are people on both sides who want it, or who think they want it, or who think it will make them heroes, and those people have guns.

We're pretty close to the last battle now. We have dead cops (and a cop's color barely matters, he or she is white to the eyes behind the gun.) We have Donald's Trump's assurance that we have a big problem called "political correctness," which means America won't be great again until we can call black people whichever insulting name we think is the funniest.

See it all as one long war, and it becomes clear.

After the Civil War, the Black Army has won a great battle. They are free, just like everyone else.

That cannot be borne. The White Army counterattacks. Jim Crow is born. The White Army wins that one.

The Black Army performs what military people call a "flanking maneuver." They can't face the White Army head on, not in the South, so they sweep around its flank, looking for freedom in the great industrial cities of the North. In a battle fought on two fronts, the Black Army defeats the White Army in the civil rights struggle.

Faced with this stunning defeat, the White Army retreats. They abandon the cities to the Black Army and build impregnable strongholds in the suburbs.

There are skirmishes. The Black Army sometimes attacks and conquers a suburb, and the White Army withdraws further, bulldozing cornfields to build another stronghold, further from the city.

Sometimes, elements of the White Army raid into the cities, retaking neighborhoods their grandparents lost to the Black Army. The lifestyle sections of newspapers celebrate these successful raids, calling the retaken neighborhoods "up and coming" or "gentrified."

There are turncoats and traitors, and sellouts. People cross the line for love or money. Hearing people say Barack Obama is America's "first black president" you see how deep the division really runs.

Barack Obama is half-black. His mother was white and his father was black, but he is a black man, because that is what the rules say. If your mother is Italian and your father is Jewish, we say you are half-Italian and half-Jewish, but if either parent is black, we say you are black. The only people who say "biracial" are inner-city grade school teachers and white women who have had a child with a black man.

And now, once more, we stare at each other from behind barricades, ready for the next battle. Both sides are better armed than ever before and a few shots have been fired by both sides.

Maybe no retreat is possible. A thousand voices tell us to stand our ground, to kill. I think soon, maybe no lives will matter.

✪✪✪

August 8, 2016

Who Dies for America?

The young man on whose grave the nation dances had the last name Khan. Not Cohen. Not Cohan.

Cohen is a Jewish name. Cohan is Irish. Jewish boys named Cohen, unable to get into some American colleges, called "Christ killers" in the streets, went ashore at Normandy. Irish boys named Cohan, the Gaelic still thick on their lips, bled to death from belly wounds at Shiloh. Back home in New York, they still faced "No Irish Need Apply" signs.

The despised hillbillies of Appalachia left their blood on Iwo Jima. Georgia's crackers, never out of their home count before, died screaming at Khe Sanh.

Black men who had seen their uncles hanging from trees joined and fought the Kaiser. Their sons, still likely to be lynched for looking too long at a white woman, fought in World War II. Japanese-American boys left families in American concentration camps to fight as a World War II outfit they called "The Purple Heart Regiment."

Despised "Redskins'" baffled the Japanese with their code talk. Mexican-Americans used to being called "greasers" came out of Texas to fight in Korea.

Chink. Jap. Kike. Wop. Mick. Polack. Spic. Coon. Redneck.

They heard it all on the streets of their hometowns, in their schools, at their jobs, from people who called themselves leaders.

It's still going on. The ugly names.

Camel jockey. Rag head. White trash. Homo. Project rat.

But they'll go, some of them will.

48

They are the ones America likes least. They are jokes, locked out of every promise, laughed at, hated as casually as you hate the cockroach you see in your kitchen.

But they'll go, some of them will.

Pushed away by people who mouth the word "democracy" in a leer of bigotry, they'll go, they'll join, they'll take up the gun. They'll die.

They're beautiful, these last-ditch American boys and girls, who, turned away at so many doors, find the door open at the recruiting station.

For the very poor among them, the uniform is the best suit of clothes they've ever owned and the food in basic training is better and more plentiful than what they had at home. The army will fix your teeth, give you eyeglasses.

Who knows why they join, these boys and girls who have more reason to hate America than they do to love America.

But they'll go, some of them will.

It used to be they'd be hated until they joined, then hated in the dusty little town around heir army base, then sent off to fight and at least they'd be heroes if they died.

Now, we don't even give them that little bit of comfort.

But they'll still go, some of them will.

August 15, 2016

I Know Some Tough Guys

I'm the kind of man who says what he means. No political correctness.

I was late for work the other day, maybe 20 minutes, and I've been late before, couple times this month.

My boss is a woman (they're all bosses these days) and she must have had a fight with her boyfriend, or it's her "special" time of the month, or maybe she's not getting enough of the old innee-outtee, if ya know what I mean.

Anyway, whatever, ya know. But she made a big deal out of me being late, again, like I wasn't the smartest guy in the place.

I knew what she was trying to pull.

So, I told her, "I know some tough guys. My buddy Ray, he owns a lotta guns, ya know. Lives in a house out in the 'burbs and he reads sniper magazines.

"Maybe I oughta have Ray come down here and take care of you so this place gets run right," I said.

Well, I got fired because they fire everybody who speaks up to the woman bosses. It's this political correctness crap.

She called the cops, too. Women are always calling the damn cops on men. It's this feminist crap.

And I got arrested and went to court and the judge musta been 60 and she probably hasn't had any lovin' since 1978.

And she started telling me I can't just threaten people.

"I know guys who own a lotta guns," I told her. "One of them was in the Army Reserve. Maybe I oughta get a couple of those guys to come down here and blow you right off of that bench."

So, now I'm doing 120 days in the house of corrections because the court system is rigged.

I'm in the chow line and Ricky, this black guy, he cuts the line, pushes me out of the way because it's Tuesday and Tuesday is pepper steak night and Ricky likes to get to the pepper steak before it gets cold.

"I know some guys with guns," I said to him.

"I don't see any of 'em in this line," he said.

He beat me pretty bad, knocked out three of my teeth. I was unconscious when the guards pulled him off of me.

He's kind of my boyfriend now.

I guess if I had Donald Trump in here with me, I'd tell him that it's better to be a tough guy than to just know some tough guys.

✪✪✪

August 29, 2016

I'm Not a Real Man

I wish I supported Donald Trump.

If you think about it, I should.

I'm a 59-year-old workingman who grew up in the Midwest. My wages have been stagnant for a number of years now. I take my hat off when I'm watching a parade and the flag passes. My grandparents were legal immigrants. I don't own a gun, but I did when I was younger, and I'm a good shot. I can box. Black people are moving into my neighborhood. I'm a Christian.

How simple, then, to buy a Chinese-made, "Make America Great Again" hat and start talking about building walls and banning Muslims. How easy to say I want to "take America back." How much fun it would be to proclaim "All lives matter"? How restful to say welfare payments are bankrupting the country even though it isn't true and hasn't ever been true.

Saying or believing all that stuff is instant tough guy, like buying a leather jacket or a motorcycle. What sagging, slightly achy man my age doesn't want to be tough again?

Was I ever tough? I was tough enough to work my way through college and graduate school. Tough enough that I've worked since I was 14, and I've never cashed an unemployment check or a welfare check. Tough enough that I own a house. Tough enough that I don't have kids who live with other people. Tough enough that, when she got old enough that a trip to the hairdresser was difficult, I taught myself to wash and set my elderly mother's hair.

Oh, but that's not it. Tough in 2016 is a gun and a swagger and a sneer at "baby mamas." Oh, your 18 year-old daughter might be pregnant out of wedlock, but she just "made a mistake." She's not a "whore" like the black women on welfare. And you might not be married to that man you live with, but you're a Christian and you believe in "family values."

Support the police, who make more money than you do and still have a union. Support the military, where the health insurance is better than you've ever had in your life. Support the corporations who buy their way out of the taxes you have to pay.

Support everyone but yourself. Beg for another smack in the mouth. You can take it. You're tough. If you weren't tough, you'd vote for black guys or women.

Yeah. I'm not a real man. If I was, I'd be afraid of everything new, everything different, everything that makes a noise in the night or a creak in the attic.

I'm not a Donald Trump supporter. You know why? Because I'm not scared.

✪✪✪

CHAPTER THREE

The Land of Trumpin

September 12, 2016

A Peep Into the Past

Sometimes, I can't avoid it, but I try not to be nostalgic.

Sure, I miss places and people I used to know, but I fight mightily against "things were better were when I was a kid," because when a 50-plus man says that what he means is he misses being young and strong. That's why so many guys my age own so many guns, because we know we can't win fistfights anymore.

If you want to know the truth of it, "I Love Lucy" wasn't hilarious; it was stupid. Tupac Shakur wrote better lyrics than The Beatles. The cars we think of as "classic" were junkers after 50,000 miles.

You start thinking that everything was better when you were a young man, you end up being mad as hell because there isn't a two-hour prayer session at the beginning of every public school day, you start claiming that "the slaves didn't have it so bad," and you end up voting for Donald Trump.

This old guy ain't goin' out like that, yo.

Of all the improvements made in my lifetime, two stand out.

The first is the clock in your car. Back when your dashboard clock had hands, like a pocket watch, the clock stopped working two weeks after you bought the car. Right now, I'm driving a 16-year-old Ford pickup and the digital dash clock is accurate to the minute.

And the second is Peeps, those marshmallow chicks people eat at Easter.

I love those things. When I was a kid, they were yellow, they were chicks and they were overly sweet. That was it for choices.

Last week, my wife, who knows I love Peeps, came home with maple brown sugar Peeps dipped in white chocolate. There are Halloween Peeps shaped like tombstones and chocolate-flavored Peeps and raspberry Peeps.

Peep technology has exploded in my lifetime and, best of all, they're still made in the USA.

I don't think most people think about either dashboard clocks or Peeps. You want to know what time its, you look at the dashboard clock. If you want to buy Fourth of July Peeps shaped like stars and sprinkled with red and blue sugar, you can.

Instead of rejoicing in these things, we complain about football players kneeling during the national anthem. Hell, maybe the guy says a prayer while he kneels. If he's being patriotic and praying at the same time, he's qualified to be the governor of any state that produces good barbecue.

I'll be 60 next May. I will die sooner rather than later.

I will not go down sucking on the bitter lemon of nostalgia. I will not listen to the oldies station. I will not live in the gated community. I will not worship Jesus as the world's biggest spoilsport. I will not follow some orange-haired old man into hell.

September 26, 2016

They Just Steal Your Money

When a town near the city where I work as a reporter began considering a vote to authorize civic improvements, I was pretty sure how the public debate would be conducted, though I wouldn't have been so sure two decades ago.

The improvement involved a modest increase in taxes, very modest. The increase would end in 20 years, when the bond was paid.

You could make a good argument for either side, based on everything from economic development, to increased traffic, increased revenue and the dislike of new tax increases. Facts were readily available.

In general, the pro-improvement side tried to paint the new project as something town residents would enjoy as well as something that would draw in visitors who would spend money in the town.

The anti-improvement side relied on the idea that the increase would be another example of "the government stealing our money to support a bloated bureaucracy and yield to the demands of union thugs." I believe the union thugs were town police officers who would be working paid details at the construction site.

Right now, in America, there is a large and growing percentage of the population that believes that ANY money the governments obtains is "stolen and wasted." Everything is government waste. Everything is corrupt. "Lining their pockets" is a phrase that crops up often.

It's a good viewpoint to have if you don't know much but you want to sound smart anyway.

"That's what they WANT you to think," you coo when

presented with a news story. "It'll all be covered up," you say when presented with any malfeasance.

Unfortunately, if you don't believe anything, you can't do anything. Endless disbelief, like irony, is the high school student's way of seeming to know what's going on in the world.

I've been a reporter for 33 years, and I've seen plenty of waste and corruption, but I've seen plenty of things in government that are neither wasteful nor corrupt.

It's not so much that you need to believe everything is a lie as it is that you have to be able to separate the lies from the truth. Believing that everything is a lie isn't one of the ways to make that separation.

We live in the land of always and never. Guns are always good. Guns are always bad. Police are murderers. Police are always innocent. All blacks are criminals. All blacks are innocent. My party does no wrong. Your party does no right. I'm a patriot. You're a traitor.

I don't know how we got to be this kind of country, but it is perilously close to being a country that cannot be governed.

They say we're winding up to an election in America, but we're not. What we're doing is holding a wake for rational thought, a funeral for compromise and a burial for civility. They will not rise again.

October 3, 2016

Revolution in America

The Associated Press story about civil war in Syria made Page 5 of the midsize daily newspaper where I work. I'd watched the Donald Trump/Hillary Clinton debate a few days before.

There are people in America who say the tree of liberty must be watered with the blood of tyrants. There are people in America who say they will fight, with guns, to keep their guns. There are people in America who say they want a revolution to "take back their country."

It's one goddamn pleasant fantasy, is what it is. You get your gun, dress up in camouflage and defeat the government.

You do not get shot in the belly and bleed to death. Soldiers from the opposing side do not invade the lawns in your suburb and gang rape your 9-year-old daughter or murder your son. You fire a couple of shots, and prayer is restored to the schools, Hillary Clinton is hung from a sour apple tree, all the immigrants are forced to learn English, and abortion becomes illegal again.

The revolution ends before the big game starts, and cable television is free. America is great again.

The Associated Press, covering a real civil war in Aleppo, writes:

"Desperate residents describe horrific scenes in Syria's largest city and onetime commercial center, with hospitals and underground shelters hit by indiscriminate gunfire that the U.N. said may amount to a war crime."

I guess those guys won't be home in time for the big game. I bet most of the sports bars have exploded and there is a critical shortage of hot wings and potato skins. War is hell.

Their civil war has lasted for more than five years. More than 250,000 people are dead, and half the population has had to seek refuge in the nearest safe place.

If you want to get in on a real civil war, one with all kinds of gun-totin' fun, maybe you ought to head to Syria. I'm sure if you looked at Facebook for 30 minutes, you could figure out which side to join.

Go be a hero someplace else.

Here, every time someone complains about something in America, you snarl, "Why don't you go back where you came from," or "Why don't you move to some other country."

Well, why don't you leave instead? Take your guns and your snarl and go where the fighting is hot and you've got a good chance of dying. C'mon, you're a hero.

I'll stay here, and so will the Syrian-American guy who owns the gas station where I go for gas. That guy lived your dream, and he hated it so much he ran away. What a punk! Not like you. You WANT civil war.

You can't spend the rest of your life practicing your fast draw in front of the bedroom mirror while your wife's at the grocery store.

Go to Syria. They're looking for heroes.

✪✪✪

October 17, 2016

So, Which Women Can I Grab?

First of all, I haven't spent my whole life in my house, trying not to get a bruise. From the age of 14 to 26, I worked my way through school at a variety of dirty minimum wage jobs including dishwashing, bartending, janitorial work, loading dock work, a stint as a laborer on construction sites and many others. I've boxed a bit, and boxing gyms are rough places full of un-nice people. As a newspaper reporter, I've covered house fires and homicides, many of them in neighborhoods where people use bed sheets for curtains, if they have bed sheets.

There are rules in all those situations, even if the rules aren't apparent to people who are either driving by or just visiting.

I like rules. You like to know where you stand when you start, so, if you break the rules, you at least know to stand by for punishment.

One of our presidential candidates thinks the rules allow you to grab women, even if they don't want to be grabbed.

I understand that rule, but it's a little too broad. I need more instruction.

My wife says she was grabbed by a man when she was 13. That's too young, right? Still, 13 ends in "teen" and so does 19, so maybe it is all right. Twelve, though, 12 is too young, unless she looks 13, which is practically 19.

What about veterans? They got women veterans now. She's just out of the army and she's waitressing and she looks pretty hot. And it's not like she's in the army now. I think I can grab her.

A widow? Her husband got blown up serving his country in Afghanistan, but check out those legs! C'mon, grab a squeeze!

Somebody else's wife? Why not? I mean, don't try anything with MY wife, but some other guy's wife?

This isn't as hard as I thought.

Of course, you have to be rich. I'm not rich, but there are a lot of women who have a lot less money than I do. They think I'm rich. You know how often I have $100 in my pocket? A lot of times, especially on payday. You think that's not rich in some places?

When you're rich, when you have $100 on you and she's a single mother on welfare, she's gonna let you do anything you want.

And I'm not gonna grab anybody my age, either. I'll be 60 next May. Grabbing some woman my own age would be like groping my grandmother.

America's a strip club these days. Pull out the money. Everything else just comes to you.

✪✪✪

October 24, 2016

Debate Night

A man ought to talk to his wife every so often, and I mean really talk.

Women live lives we don't know anything about, so it's good to check in every now and then and try to learn something. That's if she'll tell you anything. A lot of the time she won't. I believe that the world runs on the lies — or at least the silence — of women.

I was drinking coffee this morning, and I was thinking about this column and I said to my wife, "Can you imagine what would have happened if Donald Trump had said 'the N-word' instead of what he said about women?"

I use the falsely pious phrase "N-word" because it's expected, indeed demanded, of me. If it were up to me, I'd use the real word because this "N-word" business is just another way to pretend that Rosa Parks refused to give up her seat on the bus and everything was all right in the world after that.

My wife, whom I had expected to talk, just said, "If Trump said that, there'd be riots, but you can say anything you want about women."

Nope. Trump couldn't call Jews "Christ killers" and stay in the race. Nor could he say "spic."

Riots. Legal action. Candlelight vigils. Marches.

Nope. One thing is certain. You couldn't pass off "kike" as just "locker room banter."

Oh, sure, Donald Trump may lose the election in part because of a vile thing he said about women, but he wasn't immediately dragged off his throne of redneck stupidity and made to grovel in the dirt.

I told my wife tonight that, many years ago, a boss

laughed at me over something I'd done wrong. It wasn't a big something, but his laugh let me know just how tired he was of having to supervise his social inferiors. He could do it, so he did, and he did it in front of other people.

I took it, too. I needed that job.

But 30 years later, it still burns me. That man may not be alive. If he isn't, I'm sorry I wasn't there to watch him die. That's a crude and sinful sentiment, but if he wanted to be remembered well, he should have held his laughter.

I want to watch Donald Trump lose for the same reason I wanted to watch that other man die.

A man ought to talk to his wife every now and then. And I mean *really* talk.

Women live lives we don't know anything about, but when you know what dirt they are forced to eat, you burn— especially if you're in love.

October 31, 2016

BOO!

I'm going to a Halloween party tomorrow night. My wife, Deborah, says we will dress as silent movie stars. I am supposed to shave my beard and wax my mustache into points. She will put a thick layer of white makeup on my face, like the old movie stars used to do. I will wear a black suit.

The hope is that I will look like the kind of silent movie villain who enjoyed foreclosing on family farms and orphanages. In reality, I will look like an aging newspaperman who is being booted into having fun.

Deborah will dress as the flapper/vamp silent movie star. That is exactly what she'll look like, too. If you dress her in cowboy clothes, she looks like a pretty cowgirl. If you dress her up like a vampire, she looks like a pretty vampire. If you put her in a dinosaur suit, she looks like a pretty dinosaur.

I'm not pretty, and the "me" shines through every kind of costume I wear. If you get me sufficiently dirty, I can pass for homeless, but that's about my best shot at assuming a different look.

I'm not yet happy to go to the party, but I am getting through it by focusing on the fact that I'll be drinking someone else's beer. The people throwing the party are friends of ours, and I intend to ask about the food situation today. I don't mind it if there's nothing available except for a bowl of nuts, but I'll be happier if I think there's going to be chili or a plate of meat and cheese. Also, if I know there won't be much food, I'll eat a ham sandwich before I go. Nothing is worse than trying to soak up free beer on an empty stomach. It gives me heartburn.

I considered going as Donald Trump, but there are

things I won't do for free beer. In this freewheeling year, I could have gone as Hillary Clinton, but my hips are too big for a pantsuit. And, if I went as Clinton, I'd know that people were only talking to me to avoid talking to the guy dressed as Trump.

I decided to avoid the political costumes for the same reason I'm avoiding the "creepy clown" costume. You have an obligation not to cut too close to the bone at a Halloween party.

Oh, sure, if I dressed as Trump, people would come up to me and make jokes, and the young girl dressed as a cat would say, "Oooh, Mr. Trump, don't grab ME." But the jokes wouldn't be very funny, and the girl would be too young, and I'm married, and I'd have brought into the house something I should have left in the street.

We should have left Trump in the street. A thing like that doesn't belong in any good man's or woman's house.

But we have lost any idea of the fitness of things in this century, at least in America. We cover the sin of intolerance with the mask of Jesus. We dress racism up like a cop. We dress fear up as a soldier with a gun.

We are shrill and wild and hateful. We're strung out on every damn thing from talk radio to Oxycontin. We babble and froth and bite about "wanting our country back" without realizing that we ARE America. We can't stay married, and we think sending a check every month makes us a good parent, and we think buying a gun is the same thing as being tough.

It's a good year for a Halloween party, and it's good to go as something goofy and harmless, like a silent movie star or a burrito or Dora the Explorer. There is no need for artificial fear this year. We have the real thing.

✪✪✪

November 7, 2016

One Wall Is Not Enough!

Senor Trump, he's gonna build a wall to keep Carlos and the boys in Mexico, and then native-born Americans can all get jobs on the third shift at the chicken de-boning plant.

Don't expect more than the minimum wage. The boys in charge want to make America great again, but they're not stupid enough to pay hillbillies like us more than $10 an hour.

We're gonna need more walls.

There are already walls between black and white, between city and suburb, but those walls need to be sturdier, higher and thicker.

The wall between middle class and poor is in pretty good shape, but it needs some barbed wire on top. God help us if people making $50,000 a year ever figure out how much they have in common with people making $30,000 a year.

Trump's done an excellent job of strengthening the wall between poor black and poor white and, as they could have told you in 1930 Alabama, this is the key to prosperity for rich people.

If poor whites and poor blacks ever decide to stand together, the people who run the corporations that run the country are going to have something to worry about other than how to divide the profits.

The wall between Jews and Christians was starting to crumble, but we're working on getting it back to its former glory. The good news is that the wall between Christians and Muslims came in ahead of schedule and under budget. Trump got the Christians to build that one for free!

Not that Christians don't need a wall. The wall between born again and not born again gets bigger every day. And atheists? Wall 'em off from EVERYBODY!

The wall between college educated and everyone else is in great shape. If you went to college, you're an elitist with no common sense. If you never got beyond high school, you're too stupid to vote. So sayeth both sides about each other.

There's always been a wall between men and women, but there's been a lot of tunneling under and crawling over that wall. That needs to stop. You need to build a wall between women that has only one gate, a gate men can go through when they feel like grabbing a handful, which is all a real man wants.

Gays broke their wall by insisting that their status as humans gave them the right to marry, but my guess is a Trump victory will have us slapping new bricks and mortar into that very old barrier. If we have to, we'll rebuild that wall with Bibles!

Walls between veteran and nonveteran, between on welfare and almost poor enough to be on welfare. Walls between Hispanic and white, between black and Hispanic. Get 'em up! Unity is for hippies and traitors and sissies.

The wall between gun owners and non-gun owners is well-guarded, and they'll shoot to kill!

The more walls we build, the less the people in charge have to worry about us ALL getting together, about all of us wanting jobs and good wages and a decent life.

What we know now is that we have never seen the people on the other side of the wall, but there must be something wrong with them or they wouldn't be on the other side of the wall. What the people on the other side of the wall know is that they've never seen us, but there must be something wrong with us or we wouldn't be on the other side of the wall.

America on Nov. 7, 2016. Land of the divided, home of the scared, builders of walls.

✪✪✪

CHAPTER FOUR

Roll Over and Play Dead

November 21, 2016

Leonard Cohen and Donald Trump

Most American newspapers, especially the influential ones, wrote more words about the death of singer/songwriter Leonard Cohen than their readers wanted to (or did) read.

Why?

Same reason most American newspapers blew the Donald Trump story.

The whole point of memorializing the relatively unpopular Cohen was that it showed how culturally advanced the reporter was, how he didn't like Kenny Chesney.

Despite the fact that newspaper reporters tend to make a working-class wage, newspaper reporters don't think of themselves as working class. They think of themselves as rebels, as Bohemians, as people whose idea of what to like is so advanced that they like things no one else likes.

We're reporters. We're columnists. We're editors. We can cross the yellow caution tape. We call the senator by his first name.

Despite our paychecks and the company's lousy health insurance, we will not be identified with light beer or monster trucks or evangelical Christianity or professional wrestling.

Newsrooms are places where people reinforce each other's opinion.

We knew at the beginning that Trump was going to get a few votes from gun-nut crazies and then it would be over. Editorial writers at major newspapers were horrified at the idea that poor white Christians from Oklahoma actually got to vote. Hell, those people didn't even go to college!

We blew it. We didn't blow it because we were biased

72

or because we were part of a huge conspiracy or because wee were being bribed.

We blew it because we stayed in the office too much, telling each other we were right. We blew it because we went to the press conference and not to the streets. We blew it because we don't go to karaoke night at the VFW and because we don't belong to the evangelical churches where the word of God was anti-Hillary. We blew it because we have separated ourselves from the American people.

I dislike Donald Trump intensely, but I knew his supporters, and I knew he had a lot of supporters. Up until the end of this election, I was the only one in my newsroom who thought Trump might win.

Did I think that because I'm a political savant?

No.

I thought that because a significant number of my friends are working-class people. I was born into the working class. I am working class. They are my people. I didn't leave them just because I went to college.

At some point in the campaign, almost every newspaper printed the statistic that Trump did better among people who didn't go to college than he did among people who did go to college.

But no newspaper stopped to consider that *most* Americans didn't go to college. Not going to college isn't unusual; it's *normal*. If Americans who didn't go to college want something, they've got enough votes to get it. I don't recall any newspaper making that connection.

We're the reporters. We're the columnists. We're the editors. We went to college. We call the senator by his first name.

And we got smacked in the mouth because we stayed in the office, because we went straight home at night, because none of our friends dropped out of high school, or went to vocational school or got laid-off when the Spandex factory closed.

We didn't see it coming because we weren't looking, because we were trying not to look.

Are you a reporter or a columnist? Want some advice?

Next Tuesday, go down to the VFW. It's karaoke night. Sit at the bar. Buy a beer for the Iraq War vet next to you. Let him talk. For God's sake listen. If you want to get up and sing, go ahead.

Just don't ask for a Leonard Cohen song. They probably won't have it and you won't impress anyone.

✪✪✪

December 5, 2016

Let's Punish Some People for Flying the Flag

You have a constitutional right to burn the American flag, just like you have a constitutional right to bear arms.

Patriots died for both rights. Soldiers overseas are defending your right to burn the flag. Our hero police officers stand ready to protect your right to burn the flag. The Marines who died on Iwo Jima died for your right to burn the flag.

You have a constitutional right to burn the American flag in protest. You also have a constitutional right to burn the American flag for light, for heat or just for the hell of it. You have a constitutional right to burn the flag while performing an abortion or conducting weird satanic rights.

You have a constitutional right to wave the flag at Klan rallies while saying that black people are lynchable apes. You have a constitutional right to wave the flag while saying the Holocaust never happened.

If you beat a gay man to death for being gay and then burn the American flag, you can be arrested for murder, but not for burning the flag.

If you own an American company that produces its products in overseas sweatshops, you are perfectly free to fly the flag over your American headquarters.

If you're rich and you buy a company, loot its pension plan and sell its assets, when you go out of business, your now-jobless workers will leave the plant on the last day and walk past the flagpole from which you fly Old Glory. You can then fly that flag from the stern of your yacht. The brave boys at Valley Forge died for that right.

You can fly the flag out in front of your gun store in Mississippi, and you can knowingly sell guns to a "straw buyer" who will take them north to Chicago, where they will be used to shoot teenagers. You can fly the flag in front of a payday loan business where you cheat the poor.

You can fly the flag out in front of a chicken processing plant where illegal immigrants are underpaid and pushed so hard to work faster that they frequently slip with the knife and cut off a finger. You can fly the flag over your business as you break the union, as you eliminate the pension, as you demand employees work forced overtime, as you do away with sick days, as you starve and dishonor and belittle your workers.

You can fly the flag over your retail store that offers wages so low your employees qualify for food stamps. You can fly the flag over the homeless shelter in a city where there are fewer jobs every year and the ones that are left pay minimum wage.

You can fly the flag over a day labor agency where only the most desperate men and women go for work. You can fly it over a liquor store that sells cheap beer and off-brand cigarettes and lottery tickets, all the great time-wasting tools of the poor. You can fly it over the megachurch where the congregation arrives in 10-year-old Fords and the minister drives home in a Mercedes.

Don't look up at the American flag. Look down to see what it hides, what it shades, what it excuses, what it camouflages.

Root out injustice because it dishonors the flag. Stand up against prejudice because it dishonors the flag. Insist that the flag not be flown over nests of thieves and the businesses of cheats.

You don't put the flag on your bumper. You put it in your heart.

✪✪✪

December 19, 2016

The Gift Returned

You know why I dislike Donald Trump?

Because I can remember Robert Frost reciting his poetry at the inauguration of President John F. Kennedy.

In his 80s then, Frost had written movingly of everything from winter's beauty to the death of a farm hand. He wrote a poem for the inauguration, but the light was too bright for him to read it so, as poets have done since the first of days, he spoke his own words, reciting another of his poems from memory.

Try, if you can, to picture that old lion of a poet spending his words on Donald Trump, the king of cheap, the man who gold plates everything in his house because his soul is from the dollar store.

Try, if you can, to imagine Trump magically acquiring enough discernment to know good poetry from bad, to know the difference between Kanye West and Robert Frost, to know that a linebacker's records don't matter, but the words of poets count. Donald Trump is a soft, brown sliver of decay picked out from between the pointed teeth of celebrity. Imagine him talking to a poet, a man who can stop time with his words. If Trump owns a book of poetry, it is bound in handsome leather, it is a first edition worth millions, and it is unread.

Try, if you can, to imagine Donald Trump reading a poem to himself, when no one's around, for the beauty of the words. Try to imagine Donald Trump realizing that words are bigger than he is, that three or four words, in the right order, with the right sound, are more of a palace than any grossly tacky casino, worth more than the numbers and words you write on a check.

Try to imagine Donald Trump writing a poem, a poem to a woman perhaps. Try to imagine him weighing words until he can describe the curve of her forehead, the light that walks with her into a room.

At most you can imagine him with his forehead wrinkled, asking a servant, "Hey, what rhymes with 'her butt.'"

"Fat slut, sir?" the servant helpfully responds.

Imagine Donald Trump as Winston Churchill, trying to capture the bravery of British pilots who fought the Nazis in the skies over London. Churchill, that fat elitist, growled about so much being owed by so many to so few, another old poet throwing words into the mouth of time.

"It's been, I mean, it's been a disaster up there," Trump would have said. "But those guys, the pilots, they've been great, really great."

Franklin Roosevelt, another rich man who liked poetry, told a starving America that, "the only thing we have to fear is fear itself." He had nothing left to say, but, after the words, he created millions of jobs, put food into millions of skinny bellies and hired artists to write and paint and dance.

"These failing newspapers," Trump would have said, "they write slanted stories about how people are hungry. It's so bad."

I'm writing this in New England. The trees outside are black in the moonlight. I'm going to read a little poetry to myself tonight. Robert Frost.

I dislike Donald Trump because I remember Robert Frost speaking his poetry from memory at the inauguration of John F. Kennedy, because I've heard Churchill and Roosevelt, their words still full of life, even in fuzzy old recordings.

The good poetry always wins. The good art always lasts. Poured concrete casinos crumble like sandcastles.

✪✪✪

December 26, 2016

Alt-Rightnik

There is a word, a word in Yiddish, the kind of Yiddish we speak in America, and the word is "alrightnik." An alrightnik is a person who's done well for him/herself, made some money, but is still a crude, ill-mannered slob.

Since language is always on the move, I put my head to what's going on in America and decided to change that word a little, to make it "alt-rightnik."

The alt-right is what you call Nazis today. You don't call them "Nazis" because you're talking about people who live in the suburbs, people who drive SUVs, people whose kids dance in "The Nutcracker" every Christmas season. They know the difference between merlot and pinot noir. They don't live in rental property.

And you can't call 'em Nazis because, by God, their grandfathers fought in World War II.

They're doing all right. They live far enough away from the blacks in the city. They have cable. A lot of 'em went to college. They have health insurance so when their soccer-playing son, Adam, gets hooked on heroin, he'll go to rehab instead of to jail. And they're not right-wing crazies. You see them at the megachurch or the Chili's, but you won't see 'em in bed sheets, firing up a cross on the Feldman's lawn.

They're not greasy people. They don't spend their work lives getting greasy, and they don't eat greasy food.

And a lot of them are, to be polite, bat-crap crazy Nazis. You know, goose steppers, oven operators, sieg heil sweethearts. They don't get all foamy at the mouth about the international Zionist conspiracy, but they're gonna get excited if a homegrown half-price Hitler runs for president.

Everyone thinks Donald Trump got elected by three-fingered cousin Ray-Ray out there in Lonesome Lizard, Oklahoma, but there ain't enough of those guys to elect anyone.

Most Americans don't live in the country and they don't live in big cities, either. They live in the suburbs, on the cul-de-sac, about two miles from a commercial strip that includes a 7-Eleven, a Pizza Hut, at least one dojo and, if you're far south enough, a gun store called Ray's Second Amendment.

They're white people who are doing all right, though not as good as they'd like and not as good as they were 10 years ago. They hate the government, but they'd love a government job. They "want" term limits, but they don't vote and they love their state rep. because he got the high school a new tennis court.

You can't win without them, or you can't win if they're not willing to look the other way while you herd the real bigots down the road to lynchland. They live in suburbs where there hasn't been a murder in 15 years, but they're armed to the teeth and waiting for drugged-up Negros from the city to try and rape their wives. Then the lead's gonna fly.

They're all right and they're alt-right and, when the killing starts, it won't be their fault. They'd vote for Jim Crow, if some legislator would just have the sense to call it "The Family, Property and Neighborhood Rights Defense Act."

They'll let America go fascist before they'll let it go socialist because socialism never delivers on its promise of equality, but fascism always delivers exactly what it promises.

They're the "good Germans," and it won't be their fault. They'll just stand there and watch it happen.

✪✪✪

January 2, 2017

Trump's World! Excellent! Party On!

So, Donald Trump, who's, like, leader of the free world and stuff, goes on Twitter and says, in part, "Thought it was going to be a smooth transition — NOT!"

Pure "Wayne's World."

The reference is from a popular movie and "Saturday Night Live" skit from the late Cocainic Period. In other words, maybe 700 slang waves out of date.

Still, you can't blame the old guy for trying. He's rich. He's got a hot young wife. He's got a jolt of nuclear Viagra under his belt. He's gonna reach for cool. It's like that time your Uncle Ray, the one who got rich in the used mobile home business, showed up at your sweet 16 party in a Rocawear jacket.

You wanted to die — obvie!

Oh, hell, I knew it was going to be bad when the morons got their president. I just figured it would be presidential bad, statesman bad, even corporate-boardroom bad. I figured the money chimp in charge would puff himself up with pride and start using big, rolling words, or at least shorter, tougher words.

NOT!

Is this what we get?

I can hear the negotiations now.

Trump: "You have to stop fiddling with your currency."

Chinese Ambassador: "I don't think there is a way we can do that."

Trump: "WAY!"

I'm not looking forward to the collapse of the American economy because I'm six years from retirement. But I'll tough it out. I'm pretty healthy. I could easily work until I'm 75. Besides, the men in my family tend to die in their 60s, so I don't feel all that threatened.

And I'll forgive Trump for sounding crazy grandpa during the debates. It's a lot of pressure for a guy, a debate. This is particularly true if the guy isn't used to saying presidential stuff. For most of his career, Trump's been able to get ahead by saying, "Screw the contractors. Don't pay 'em." And "You're fired." And, of course, "You want green card? We make boom-boom, and I get you green card."

You want to know who our next president is? Go to your local newspaper webpage, bring up any story about your mayor, and scroll through the comments.

Sooner or later, you'll find this comment.

"Mayor Smith has done SO much for our city! Oh, wait a minute, I forgot. He's done NOTHING!"

Laugh when you read that comment. Laugh loudly and laugh for a long time, because that's who is in charge now.

By the way, the name given by the commenter will be "Second Amendment Sam," "Citizen Journalist" or "Term Limits NOW."

It's not so much that Trump is so full of snark. It's just that it's such bad snark, such kid-in-the-back-of-the-class-who-never-takes-off-his-coat snark.

The best way to learn how to cover politics is to cover town politics in the small places, the little towns where character is written in very dark ink.

I was covering a town council race in one of those places years ago, and there was a candidate's debate in the Methodist church. One of the guys running was Donald Trump, but younger.

A guy in the crowd asked the incumbent a softball question, and Trump Boy was on it like ugly on an ape.

"That guy's a plant!" He yelled victoriously. "He's your campaign manager! You got him here asking you the easy questions because you can't answer the hard questions!"

82

"He's not my campaign manager," the incumbent said.

Messengers were dispatched to the Town Hall. Soon enough, they returned with the incumbent's nomination papers. His campaign manager was, as he said, not the fellow who'd asked him the question. I enjoyed my job that night, and I enjoyed working election night, when Trump Boy lost.

Which is not what happened this year. Get used to it, and keep laughing for as long as it lasts. Say it with me:

Trump's World! Party on! Excellent! Nuclear holocaust!

✪✪✪

No Socks, No Class

Joseph "Joey No Socks" Cinque is at best a lower-level mob associate, although someone thought he was important enough to shoot in 1980. And, of course, Joey No Socks was invited to Embarrassment-Elect Donald Trump's New Year's Eve party.

Why?

Because once you've installed golden toilets in your house and married an immigrant who lets people take naked pictures of her for money, the next logical step is to invite a cheap little thief to your New Year's Eve party. Donald Trump's unerring instinct for sleaze is amazing, as highly developed as a hunting dog's delicate nose. If it's greasy and covered in either vomit or gold, Trump grabs it like it's the tender parts of a woman he's just met.

The man does have standards, though.

Cinque's white and, anyway, the old Italian-American Mafia is kinda cute. And they're white.

You're not gonna see some gold-toothed, low-pants-wearin', crack-slingin' black gangsta at one of Trump's parties. Better to get what one of what my bartender father used to call "the oil and vinegar crowd." Trump woulda thought my Pop was cool, too. Pop wore a pinkie ring, and once got arrested for stopping a bar fight by punching the police chief's son in the mouth. Pop, I might mention, was white.

Yeah. You're not gonna catch the Trumpanzee swingin' with any boyz from the hood, no matter how many people they've killed or how many times they've been shot. Ditto your Asian and Hispanic gang members. Those people are thugs, like those Black Lives Matter thugs and those black-people-shot-in-the-back-by-cops thugs.

Naah. What you want at your bloated fatback New Year's Eve party is somebody who has some thrillingly dangerous associations, but who is, by God, white.

You don't want to hang out with any black academics, either. Most of them are still honked off about that whole "slavery thing." They never forget. If you want to hang out with smart black guys, make it Ben Carson, who is probably crazy.

Donald Trump does with his money and celebrity what your idiot cousin Donnie would do with the money if he won a $10 million lottery. Donnie would go to the strip club every night, and he'd throw money at the girls. He'd buy a Mercedes with wire wheels, and he'd have gold toilets in his house. Hell, Donnie would MARRY a stripper, preferably one with a sexy foreign accent and a burning desire to remain in America.

Eventually, Donnie would get addicted to cocaine, and then crack. He'd either die or burn away all his money, and he'd wind up in prison, sleeping on a mattress thinner than his stripper wife's promise to love him forever.

If you know Donnie at all, you know he's good to hang around with as long as he's poor. He works. He'll help you move. He'll drive you to the airport and back you up in a bar fight. If he wins $10 million, he may embarrass himself for a while, but he will eventually go away. One way or the other. It's Donnie's last tip of the hat to civilization.

Not so for Donald Trump. He's not going anywhere. He doesn't even have the excuse that he doesn't know how to act because he was poor all his life and then won a bunch of money.

No, the Trumpanzee has always been rich, but none of that inherited or earned wealth could keep him from running back to sleaze like a dog returning to it's own vomit.

✪✪✪

February 6, 2017

It's Real People Now

I know a guy. I don't know how he votes because I was raised not to ask, but I know he is the first generation of his family to be born an American citizen.

From time to time, we go out for a beer, but never more than two or three because he is married with a six-month-old daughter, and I am tremendously afraid of displeasing my wife. By the time he is over 50, any man who wants at least one crying woman at his funeral ought to be afraid of displeasing his wife.

We go to one of those veterans clubs that has a bar. We go there because you can smoke in the bar, because domestic beer is $1.75 a draft, and because he is a veteran. It's quiet and the television is always tuned to either Fox News or a ballgame. He likes ballgames, we are both newspaper reporters, and neither one of us likes Fox News.

And we sit in a cloud of my cigar smoke, and we talk.

He has an old aunt who came here quite a few decades ago, and who found her bit of the American Dream in a garment factory. She stitched and her husband worked in some other kind of factory, and they paid rent, and raised children.

And her husband died, and she is old now, no longer strong-eyed or quick-fingered enough to sew, and who works when they're 80 anyway? You'll sometimes meet an 80-year-old librarian in some sleepy small town library, and lawyers sometimes go on that long, but if you are bent over a machine or if you are working on the foundation crew, you don't last that long.

She gets her Social Security. She also gets food stamps

and government help with her heating bill in the winter.

She is a legal immigrant, and a citizen.

"I don't think they'd do anything to her," he said to me the other night as the TV blared Donald Trump's speaking. "She's completely legal. But she's an immigrant, and she's on government assistance."

His aunt is lucky. She is legal, of course, but she is also white and Christian, two things that become more of a test of our fitness to live every day.

So, she'll probably be fine.

Unless some white guy nearly her age, some new bigot who's oiled his way into government's back door, decides that she will not be all right.

After all, he'll tell us, can you really expect to come to this country, even legally, with no skills and wind up eating off the taxpayer's dime? Why didn't she have a BETTER job, this old woman? Why didn't she take night classes, and better herself, go to college and then to law school? Why did she just work her little stupid job all those years, and then start begging the successful Americans for food? If this is why these people come here, to fail and then leech off the system, then maybe they should be kicked outta the system.

I bought the third and last round, because he has that new baby at home. We drank it while Fox News trumpeted the triumph of the Trumpanzee.

"It's like it's about real people now," he said to me.

"Yeah," I said. "It's not Facebook memes or stick figures anymore. It's people."

Which is what history will remember Americans saying on that last night before the hammer fell.

✪✪✪

February 13, 2017

Donald Trump's Ghost Dance

In 1890, in the American West, out there where the streams are fast and clear and the rivers are slow and muddy, a Native American named Wovoka started preaching the Ghost Dance.

It wasn't a good time to be Native American, as it hasn't been since. The buffalo were gone. Ravaged by disease, hungry, drunk and preyed upon, the remainder of the people squatted forlornly on pieces of land the white people didn't need for a pipeline yet. There was no longer any way to live the way they used to live just a generation ago. In this manner, they were much like people in the Midwest whose fathers worked in the auto plant, but the plant's gone, so they clerk at the 7-Eleven.

Wovoka's theology was pretty simple, as is the theology of many right-wing Christians.

If you danced the Ghost Dance, if you integrated that way of prayer into your life, things would get better. Things would get hugely better.

Did they listen to Wovoka? Sure they did. They didn't have much left to do but dance, the way unemployed white people now don't have much to do but read Breitbart. It's better than nothing.

If you danced the Ghost Dance, Wovoka said, the white people would go away and the buffalo would return. Things would be the way they once were, back when things made sense.

In America, where it's lonely at the top and crowded at the bottom, Donald Trump preached the Ghost Dance.

It wasn't a good time to be white in America, or so

people said. You had to go to college or trade school or junior college to get almost any kind of good job. You couldn't just step out of high school and into a unionized factory that made toasters or cars or curling irons. Ravaged by painkillers, pension-less and working jobs that didn't include health insurance, the people worried that the government would encourage flag burning and kill you for praying, instead of the other way around.

Trump's theology was simple, as was the theology of Wovoka.

If you danced the Ghost Dance, Trump said, the black people would go away and the factories would return. Also, the Muslims would go away, and most of the Mexicans and the gays. Things would be the way they once were, back when things made sense.

If you danced, and if you chanted, "libtard sheeple," and posted Facebook memes showing a pistol and the words, "THIS is my president," the Chinese would quit making iPads, or at least they'd open an iPad factory in your town, out of respect for how sincerely you danced.

It was a beautiful thing to believe, and you rose to your feet and danced in the glow of the television or the computer screen, as the Native Americans danced in the light of the fires.

The beauty of Wovoka's theology was that it was just for Native Americans.

The white people wouldn't get anything good out of it, and they weren't meant to get anything good. They would go away. They would be destroyed. The Native American culture would be the only culture left. And the buffalo would come back. It was a theology that promised good things only to some people.

Wovoka's Ghost Dance didn't work. The white people didn't go away. The buffalo did not return. It was just a dancing dream in the firelight.

Wovoka's theology wasn't a theology. It was just a

dream of living the old ways in the old days. Trump's theology isn't a theology, either. It's just a denial that there is anything out there, out beyond the weak light of a small fire, and a clumsy dance.

CHAPTER FIVE

Side-of-the-Mouth Stories

January 18, 2016

The Old-Guy Diss

I'm 58 years old. On the plus side, I've still got all my hair. On the minus side, I don't have all my teeth. On the plus side, I can still wear sport coats I bought 20 years ago. They're tweed. Tweed lasts. I can't box anymore because of my right knee, which will no longer allow me to pivot the way you have to if you're going to throw a good right hand. Age is winning, but on the right night, I can feel like I'm holding the years to a tie.

About three weeks ago, I was in a social situation with two 30-something fellows who were discussing their college years.

"I was a barista in college," one of them said.

"So was I," the other guy said.

A barista is the person who makes coffee at a Starbucks coffee place. At the diner I go to, the person who makes the coffee is named "Rosaria" and I do not believe she calls herself anything other than, "someone who owns a diner."

"I still know how to make all those drinks," one of the former baristas said to the other, and the two of them were off on a magical memory tour of lattes with soy milk, double foam, a caramel drizzle and a dusting of cinnamon or nutmeg or garlic.

I let them finish.

"When I was in graduate school, I was a bartender," I said. "I still remember how to break up bar fights with a baseball bat."

Geez, it felt good when they both stopped talking.

It was the classic old-guy diss. Lattes, schmattes. Try using a worn Louisville Slugger to back down a belligerent laborer who has drunkenly decided that some other fellow is "looking at" his girlfriend.

I do remember how to use a baseball bat to break up a bar fight. The trick is to keep the bat in motion at all times. Don't swing it, shake it. And make sure the other guy doesn't step inside the arc of the bat. A baseball bat is a long-range weapon. The guy on the thick end of the bat is at an extreme disadvantage but, if he steps inside the arc and grabs the bat, the two of you end up struggling over the damn thing, and you lose all your power in the relationship.

I didn't play baseball in either grade school or high school, so my introduction to the bat came late, and only as a weapon. Breaking up fights terrified me, too, since you never know if the belligerent drunk is carrying a pistol.

Usually, all I had to do was come out from behind the bar with the bat in my hand, shake it shoulder high a couple of times and the belligerent drunk's friends (they all have a lot of friends) would drag him out of the place.

Was it worth it, to be terrified all those years ago, for $20 a shift and tips? Was it worth it just to be able to hand out the old-guy diss to a couple of former baristas?

No. It wasn't worth it, not at all. I was scared and acting tougher than I was, trying to get through grad school on short money. It was awful. I'm glad I remember that, too. If I slide into nostalgia, I'll really be an annoying old guy.

January 11, 2016

I Hate 'Downton Abbey'

It is his lordship's tweed that drew me in, I suppose. I am a great wearer of tweed and, when my wife decided we would watch the British series "Downton Abbey," I was first struck, and then enraptured, by the clothing of the men in the series, which is set among the English aristocracy in the years before and after World War I.

"Look at that tweed," I would say admiringly to my wife as his lordship strode off across the fields or lounged in a huge armchair, reading The London Times.

Gray tweed. Brown tweed. Green tweed. Green tweed with a faint red stripe. I was in love.

In the beginning of the series, all was well. The family was rich landed gentry. Their house was huge. Their servants were plentiful and respectful. They lived by an iron code of conduct. Their tweed was gray and well-fitting.

Unfortunately, the series was set during a "time of change." Writers love to set stories during a time of change because it gives them a free plot. The writer establishes characters and, bang, a war breaks out or there is a huge social upheaval. Women want to vote. Servants no longer wish to serve. Butlers grow weary of buttling. Unsuitable couplings occur. The younger generation falls away from tweed.

"They're ruining the show," I said to my wife as his lordship's family began producing out-of-wedlock children, as one of his daughters married the chauffeur, and as the footmen became surly and seemed to smirk as they brought the tea.

"What's wrong?" my wife said.

"Everything's changing," I said. "No one's happy."

94

My wife explained to me (rather slowly, I thought) that the series had to have a plot.

"Couldn't it just be that maybe the episodes focus on the planning of the yearly hunt ball or on the butler forgetting to order new tweed for his lordship?" I said.

"So, the show would just be about nothing?" my wife said. "Like 'Seinfeld'?"

"Yes," I said. "It would be like 'Seinfeld,' except the characters would all wear tweed and they wouldn't be whiny, sexually inept New Yorkers I'd like to hit with a tire iron."

Last weekend, we watched the first episode of the last season of "Downton Abbey." I'm not sure, but I think the under butler shot two nuns and a duke impregnated one of his lordship's prize cattle.

When television and movie script writers set their stories in a time of change, my favorite character is always played by the oldest actor in the cast, the one whose character is invariably whipped bloody because he can't "accept change."

I can accept change. I've been a reporter for 30 years and newsrooms are change-y places. One murderous cackle of the police scanner and I'm down in the projects, watching them put the victim's body into the ambulance.

Change is fine. I don't wear a holstered pistol to the grocery store because it's not 1876 anymore. I won't vote for Donald Trump because I know America isn't a "white man's country" anymore.

I'll keep watching "Downton Abbey," but only for the tweed. Tweed never lets me down.

❂❂❂

February 15, 2016

The Opioid Crisis Is Crap

I live in a poverty-stricken former factory town of about 85,000 people. We are, they tell us, in the middle of an "opioid crisis." They tell us this because people in nearby suburbs, white people with a full set of teeth, have begun to overdose. You could buy heroin in my city in the 1950s. We're used to the junkies.

Our state reps are eager to declare an "opioid crisis" because it will mean an ocean of federal money for "education," which will enable their worthless cousin with the social work degree from Second Rate State to get a job with a grant program in the schools.

I'm not so sure.

I'm told by a thousand mouths that the "opioid crisis" is the fault of Big Pharma, which gets people addicted, or doctors, who get people addicted, or the price of heroin, which is cheap, or the purity of heroin, which is excellent. I'm told it's because drugs are "everywhere" in poor neighborhoods. Six months ago, cops busted a heroin house I can see from my kitchen window, so I am not writing this from the lofty perspective often attributed to newspaper columnists. I told you. I live in a poor place.

So, I'll tell you what I do know.

In the course of my life, I've been friends with a number of people who kicked one addiction or another. One of my friends, an alcoholic and amphetamine user, pieced together 10 years sober before the liver he'd outraged for decades stopped working. It killed him.

Not one of those people ever told me he was a drunk or a junkie because there were liquor stores near his house or bars in his neighborhood or because there was an open bar at his cousin America's wedding reception. Not one has ever told me his doctor was responsible. The only people who tell me those stories are drunks who are still drinking or junkies who are still using.

The people I know who have continued not to drink or use tell me stories that begin with "I."

"I am an alcoholic."

"I am a junkie."

The stories go from "I" to "me," a dismal litany of failure, terror and shame.

But the stories are studded with "I" and "me," flags of pride, a bearing of the burden, a tattered wish to get it the hell over with and face the truth.

Ask the drunks. Ask the junkies. Recovery doesn't work until you say it's "your" problem. Mommy and Daddy out there in the 'burbs may need a reason why their 16-year-old soccer player started spiking up, but the real junkies know that excuses and reasons are crap. Excuses and reasons help you use. They don't help you quit.

As we subtly shift the idea of addiction from being an internal problem to a disease we caught from someone else, the newspaper editorial writers and the state reps. find more reasons to use the word "victim." They are happy.

And it's crap.

✪✪✪

March 21, 2016

Smile Like Mona Lisa

They stand in line outside the homeless shelter I pass on my way home from work, smoking, most of 'em, waiting for the 5 p.m. opening.

I know many of them from stories I've written. They lounge in the public library where my mother used to work. They panhandle outside the newspaper office where I work, outside of the breakfast and lunch joint down the street, outside of the bar I've been going to for 20 years.

I'm predictable. I'm good for some change.

Today, there was a guy I'd never seen before, but I'm pretty sure I know his story.

He was young, clean. Usually that kind of guy just got bounced by a girlfriend, and he's not from here so he doesn't have family or friends he can stay with for a while. Those guys don't look concerned. They'll go back to her tomorrow, apologize, promise to straighten up. It usually works.

I know I'm supposed to hate them because they're smoking $7-a-pack cigarettes instead of putting that money toward a security deposit. I wish the poor would spend their money wisely, but I know it's hard to think ahead when you're waiting for the homeless shelter to open.

There was a heavily built woman outside today, wearing a bulky tan coat, smiling a little bit of a secret smile, listening to the skinny guy next to her, who may have been singing the old, sweet song. Then again, he could have been singing some much worse lyric. There are drug dealers working the streets round here and, after dark, the sidewalk in front of the library blooms with street whores.

I used to have bad jobs when I was a young man. It

didn't make much difference that they were bad jobs either. I lived with my parents and was just earning college money.

Generally, there was a back door to the places where I worked, always made of steel with a very small window high up on the door. The window always had wire mesh embedded in the glass.

We'd stand out there and smoke on our breaks, a rough-looking bunch on some rough minimum-wage job, hotel maids and cooks, janitors, loading dock workers, whatever the job description was on the other side of that particular steel door.

I sang the old, sweet song out there a time or two and got a secret smile back. We all laughed and smiled out there on those 15-minute breaks that were always interrupted at the end by a boss. I don't remember why we laughed or smiled. We sure as hell weren't stupid enough to like the job.

And we looked, I know I looked, just like those people I see every day at the shelter. We couldn't really afford to smoke, either, though all of us smoked. We were foolish and untidy and those of us who weren't in school were probably going to be smoking outside some steel door for the rest of our lives. The last good thing we had before we went back in was that smile.

May 16, 2016

Massachusetts Murderer Not a Killer in the Ring

My father used to say, "Time is so everything doesn't happen all at once. Distance is so everything doesn't happen to you."

He may have been quoting something he'd read, or he might have made it up. Maybe it was something he'd heard in some bar, a ways back down the road.

I thought of that when a 28-year-old Taunton, Massachusetts, man named Arthur DaRosa went on a stabbing rampage in that small city. He killed two people before being shot to death by an off-duty sheriff's deputy. He did these things in a house and a shopping mall, on the same night, 30 minutes from the newspaper office where I work.

But in January, I watched DaRosa fight in the Golden Gloves. He fought at 165 pounds, and dropped a split decision to a fighter named Ayoule Tom Jones, out of Providence, Rhode Island.

I found my story from that night. I called the DaRosa/Jones fight the "fight of the night." Jones was a better boxer, but DaRosa was fairly hard to hit, and in the second round both men punched nearly continuously. By the third, my notes tell me Jones was up on his toes, hitting a very game DaRosa who was, I write in my notes, falling behind. "Good, good fight," my notes say. It was a close fight with a lot of action.

Fight of the Night.

Some guys will meet a famous organized crime guy in a bar in New York, and spend the rest of their lives telling people, "He was sittin' right next to me," like it makes them a famous criminal, too.

It doesn't.

My old man was right, of course. At the fights, the distance between Arthur DaRosa and I wasn't very big, and we were there at the same time. What saved me from being killed by him is that I was not in the same place at the same time when he began killing people.

That's not much to hang your life on, but it'll do.

Every source I've seen says DaRosa had some kind of mental problem, and had been treated. On Facebook, where time and distance don't matter much, DaRosa is being used to prop up anti-gun control arguments because a guy with a gun shot him and stopped his rampage.

Over the decades, I've watched fighters in the ring who were or later became professional criminals. Some of them are dead. Some are in jail. A few of them ended up killing someone. It doesn't make me tough. I'd have been afraid to sit next to most of those guys on a bus.

I saw Arthur DaRosa fight a hell of a fight, and a boxing ring is a good place to give your devil some exercise, tire him out, and make him too sleepy to cause trouble. Of course, some devils never get tired.

Everybody's a victim in this one. Even the cop who shot DaRosa may find he has acquired a hard-to-tire devil. The bell is ringing and it's time to come out for the next round.

May 23, 2016

How to Act in the Men's Room

Since I am assured the bathroom down at my favorite seven-stool, five-table, no-we-don't-have-a-blender bar is about to be overrun by female-to-male transgender freedom fighters, I figured I'd help 'em out a little bit.

First of all, I assume most of them will just buy the clothes and get the haircut. And then, when they go into my men's room, they'll just skitter into a stall, like I'm sure my wife does.

They're going to miss the fun and camaraderie of public urination. That's why I urge people who want to become men to get the surgery. It's expensive and it hurts, but I really can't stand with you until you stand next to me, if you know what I'm saying.

If you get re-plumbed, you've already broken one of the man rules by going to the doctor voluntarily. If you're a real man, then you go to the doctor only when you've got a piece of metal embedded in you somewhere or your wife makes you go.

But let's say you have gone, and you are now a physical man. You're gonna want to belly up to the urinal.

First of all, those "no eye contact" and "no talking" rules are for guys who have never been in the military or in prison, or never had an outside job where the boss didn't provide bathroom facilities.

For men, the whole world is our bathroom. We're like dogs. We're not embarrassed by anything that might happen or any vile sounds or smells we might produce. In fact, if you just got the plumbing re-done, I recommend you start by relieving yourself outside. Live the freedom. Another good place to begin is one of those sports stadiums where, instead of urinals, they have a long trough and you stand shoulder-to-shoulder, talking about that last home run. I once saw a guy stand at just such a sports stadium trough, eating a slice of pizza with his right hand while his left remained out of sight. I couldn't give him any lip about it, either. I was smoking a cigar.

You don't have to wash your hands when you're done, either. To be honest, most of us don't. I told you, we're not embarrassed by anything. You can check your hair in the mirror before you go — in case that nice-looking girl at the bar lets you buy her a drink. She'll notice if your hair looks good, but she'll never know you didn't wash your hands, so why bother?

As to what you say to the guy next to you, talk about that girl at the bar. Ask him what the line is on the game. You don't have to specify which game, either. He'll know.

If you can't think of anything else, say, "You don't buy beer, you just rent it." He'll laugh. Trust me. I've heard that line 416,000 times and I've laughed every time.

You ready? Tell ya what. There are probably five guys in there. Let's just go out by the dumpster.

You get any on these shoes and I'll kill ya.

June 13, 2016

Want an Orange Soda? Good Luck.

I like orange soda. I like grape, too.

It's something an 8-year-old boy would like, and it embarrasses me sometimes. At the newspaper where I work, the newsroom is full of guys drinking energy drinks and sports drinks and coconut water and pomegranate nectar. Me, I got a 12-ounce glass bottle of Fanta Grape on my desk.

I like the Mexican Fanta, too. The Mexican one is sweeter and grapier. Apparently, sweet soda is like cocaine now. The cartel has to mule it in from below the border. Donald Trump's wall is probably going to put a stop to that and I'll end up drinking that flavored seltzer, the kind that says "grape" on the bottle but has only a suggestion of grape flavor. The grape-flavored seltzer is like the cocaine they sell in suburban high schools compared with the cocaine they sell in bad neighborhoods.

It's likewise in the stores, too. Forget the big "convenience" stores, where they've got a wall full of Guava Energy Triple X Energy Fizz, but you can't get a bottle of orange soda.

You wanna get the real grape and orange soda? If you do, you gotta go to a corner store in a crappy neighborhood. In those stores, the owner's not from America, they sell single cigarettes from under the counter and you can buy Fourth of July fireworks, illegally, in February.

Here's a tip. If the store has an "EBT Welcome" sign in the window and they sell those cheap cigarettes that burn real fast, they'll have real orange soda, in a glass bottle.

If the store has a counter designed to be too high for robbers to jump over and sells toilet paper one roll at a time, they're gonna have grape soda.

In fact, the second kind of store will have grape cigars. They'll also have grape bubble gum, grape vodka, grape Popsicles and grape incense. There is apparently a great need among the urban poor to experience the wonders of artificial grape flavoring. It's not an ethnic thing, either. Grape-flavored anything is equally popular in poor black, poor white and poor Hispanic neighborhoods.

Orange and grape sodas were socially acceptable when I was young. That's how I got started. Back then, people would give the stuff to kids. Parents today fear the "sugar rush." When I was a boy, if you got all cranked up on soda, your old man just told you to go outside and play. Sometimes, he'd throw you half a buck, and you'd go down to the corner and get another soda.

These days, parents with a degree in marketing and shaky nonunion jobs are funneling acai berry juice into their kids, while I'm forced into an increasingly dangerous series of lousy neighborhoods, just to get a bottle of the sweet stuff from Mexico.

They used to sell grape soda in every working-class neighborhood. Of course, when was the last time you saw a working-class neighborhood?

✪✪✪

July 11, 2016

Achoo! God Bless You!

The man who sits at the desk to my left sneezed today, in the afternoon, maybe 2 p.m.

"God bless you," I said.

Actually, I didn't so much say, "God bless you," as much as I mumbled, "Bless ya."

He didn't say, "Thank you."

A lot of people don't say, "Thank you," when I mumble, "Bless ya."

I'm sure some clever statistician with a big roll of grant money in his pocket knows how often people say, "God bless you," after other people sneeze. And I'm sure he's worked out the coefficient of how many people say, "Thank you," in return.

The ceremonial exchange of phrases after a sneeze is one of those "Marc, what do you say?" moments from my childhood.

I'd be out with my pop and someone would sneeze or say, "Merry Christmas," or hold a door open for me or give me something and I'd be standing there like a little dope and Pop would look at me and say, "Marc, what do you say?" and I'd say, "Thank you" or "God bless you" or "Excuse me" or "Please" or "Merry Christmas" or whatever fit the situation.

I'm still saying all those things at the proper times, too, but I'm falling down on sneeze etiquette.

I'm not the only one, either.

I've noticed in the last few years that you can sneeze and people won't say anything at all. I think that's why I've started mumbling, "Bless ya," instead of delivering the full, rounded, "God bless you." A couple more years and I'll be mumbling, "Bluhya," and people will think I just sneezed.

And it's my own fault. As "God bless you" became more and more rare, I gave in. I shortened what I said and I started mumbling. I'm part of the damn problem.

And what about God? How do you think he feels in heaven, listening sadly to the dwindling number of post-sneeze prayers we send up?

"Bluhya?" he mutters. "What the hell does that mean?"

The guy next to me? He has allergies. He's gonna sneeze again, probably tomorrow, in the afternoon, maybe 2 p.m.

"God bless you," I'm gonna say, not loud, but distinctly, so he can hear every word.

If he doesn't say, "Thank you," then I'm gonna look him in the eye and I'm gonna say, "What do you say?"

I'm bigger than he is.

July 18, 2016

Pokémon at Auschwitz

The Auschwitz-Birkenau State Museum, on the site of the World War II Nazi death factory, has banned visitors from playing Pokémon Go in the camp where more than 1 million people were murdered.

What stubborn, silly creatures we are, how forgetful and beautiful and foolish.

I'm on the side of the people who did the banning. Playing Pokémon Go at Auschwitz takes the bland office accusation of "inappropriate behavior" to new heights.

But look at us, we humans, so quick to heal from our terrible hurts, so fast to forget, so determined to play in a terrible world.

Memory doesn't really mean much to us, not for long. We have so little time to live. My father died 30 years ago, and I miss him, but I can't mourn the way I did the day he died. Or the year after he died.

Pokémon Go is a smartphone game, an app that allows you to capture imaginary creatures in a real-life setting. It's foolish, like professional soccer or perfume.

Every soccer ball ever made, every ounce of perfume ever bottled, is our silly little denial of death.

Who can think of death every day and manage to live? Who can mourn forever, for generations, for eternity? Life is always the same, whether created in a suburban marriage bed where there is an expectation of college for the child, or created behind a dumpster where there is no expectation of the next meal.

Grass grows inside Auschwitz. Rain falls. If the camp had not been preserved by people doing the right thing, it

108

would be a grassy hump now.

The idea behind such preservation is that, if we remember, it won't happen again. But it will, and it has. The human race is lovely and foolish and stubborn and evil and brutal and awful to look at sometimes.

We can oppose the awfulness with our belief in God, our nobility, our compassion, our stubborn urge to do right no matter how difficult.

And we can oppose it with stupid little games, sappy love songs, pet dogs, kissing, balloons and every other inconsequential, ornamental, unimportant thing ever invented by our tribe of frolickers in the face of death.

We mourn, and we dance. We lock the doors against the terrors of the night and open the windows to the summer sunshine. We lose our children to sickness, and we keep right on making love. Life is a funeral and we tell funny stories about the deceased. When you consider the age of the earth itself, humans are like those flies that live for only a day or two.

Auschwitz is a dead serious place, built to kill with the dry efficiency of a tax preparation company run by a maniacal accountant who can kill you if he doesn't approve of your deductions.

And Pokémon Go is life being ridiculous, it's beating the living hell out of death and the memories of death, if only for a little while. Keep playing. It's just about all we've got.

✪✪✪

August 1, 2016

A Beautiful Death

Men who believe in some version of Islam cut the throat of Fr. Jacques Hamel the way you'd cut the throat of a hog. He was 85, a priest celebrating Mass in a small French town called Saint Etienne-du-Rouvray. "Etienne" is the French version of the English name Stephen. St. Stephen, stoned to death A.D. 36, is the first Christian martyr.

I helped butcher a hog once. Another young man shot the hog in the head and I drew the bright blade across the dead animal's throat. We ate fresh pork tenderloin that night.

The difference between Hamel and the hog is that Hamel died a beautiful death.

In these days when the early martyrs are forgotten and when we think all death is ugly and that the Catholic churches of France are more museums than houses of worship, we forget.

The French nuns of the Sisters of the Holy Union of the Sacred Heart, who taught me when I was a boy, never forgot.

In the early 1960s, when I attended grade school, the sisters were clothed and mentally armored after the manner of the 1400s.

Above all else, they were certain. They knew we were sacks of skin stuffed with sin, but they knew that there was some light of holiness inside us, that the call to sacrifice meant so much more than just pain.

They were beautiful. They had thrown themselves down a well for God, drowned in God and woke back up again in God.

Hamel fell, bleeding out like a stuck pig, gurgling in his throat, while his executioners pranced and bellowed around

110

him.

And he opened like a rose, became a church in his own body, lay dead at the foot of the altar on which he'd sacrificed his whole life.

He was beautiful in those final seconds, the ugliness of his death just a backdrop for the soul those men couldn't touch.

Make a saint of him. He deserves it in this time when so few of us believe in the saints, so many of who died deaths that were like jewels thrown casually at the feet of God.

We've lost the poets who wrote the songs of triumphant tragedy. We've lost the painters who painted the death of saints and heroes as victories, not defeats. The worst thing about us here in Europe and America, is that we are scared of death every minute of our lives, a failing that sells everything from smoothies to free weights.

He was just an old priest in a small church, an old man with an old man's goat face and an old man's sour wine smell, and he died stuck like a pig.

A death so beautiful in its purity, it sings in the ears like hymn.

✪✪✪

August 22, 2016

Things I Learned on the Street

I'm a newspaper reporter for a midsize daily paper in an economically depressed Massachusetts city. While I'm not on the "crime beat," the paper has a small enough staff that everyone does a little bit of everything.

I like doing a little of everything. I'm also my paper's columnist, and I write this column, and you can't learn how to write a column by sitting in an office, absorbing the air conditioning.

I went to a stabbing this morning, in a shaky neighborhood. It was a pretty cheap stabbing, too. Two guys were beating up another guy, and one of them pulled a knife and cut him on the hand.

A woman standing across the street from the fight yelled, "Noooo!" That caused all three men to run away. In bad neighborhoods, victims run away, too, if they can. You handle it yourself or you don't, but you don't talk to the cops.

"Rat!" one of the men yelled at the woman as he ran away.

That is a serious thing. "Rat," passes from mouth to mouth, and being known as one comes with its own trouble.

"I yelled 'Nooo!'" she told me. "'Just hit him!'"

She wasn't directing the violence, either, just urging the men to have a little caution. People who live with violence all the time are apt to see its varieties very clearly.

I lit a cigarette. I usually smoke a pipe, but the morning was too hot for a pipe. If you light a cigarette in a poor neighborhood, someone will ask you for one. Be generous. Tobacco makes people talk.

If the victim is dead and you have to talk to a relative or friend, start by saying, "I'm sorry." If one of your co-workers told you his son was dead, wouldn't you say, "I'm sorry"?

I talked to the cops, but not too much. Cops have a very limited range of information they can give you, and they're scared to death of being misquoted. Sometimes they'll tell you more if you don't ask questions. Listen when they talk into their radios and smartphones. If you've known one of the cops long enough to consider him a friend, don't give him too much of a greeting. He may not want the other cops to know he's your friend.

By the time I'd finished one cigarette and given away three more, I had a notebook full of quotes and enough information to write.

Don't leave a crime scene too fast. Put your notebook in your pocket and stand around a while. If there's a corner store around, go in and buy something, a bottle of soda maybe.

Do it because it's a tough place to do business and the storeowner is at least trying.

September 5, 2016

Learning to Work

I live in the city where I work, and it's a tight little city, and on my way to work, I see the kids going to school, to grade school.

The really young ones, the ones just starting the trip, are brought to school by dad or mom. Some of 'em don't even walk that steadily, they've still got a little of that wide-legged toddler walk.

And I think that, what you really start learning, on that first day in school, is how to work, how to hide yourself, how to do what someone else wants you to do.

Until then, you're a baby. You sleep when and where you want, eat when you want, go to the bathroom when you want. You can sit and look out the window for two hours in the afternoon and the only thing that happens is your mother says, "Are you sad?" and gives you a cupcake.

Is there a more beautiful sound than a mother's voice asking "Are you sad?"

School is like a job with no paycheck. You have to show up on time. You can't leave until it's time to leave. You get regular, too-short breaks. There's a teacher/boss who tells you what to do, and your fellow workers are strangers your first day on the job. You look out the window for five minutes and teacher/boss says, "Stop daydreaming" or "Pay attention."

You have to wear "appropriate" clothes. You can't take your shoes off because your feet are hot.

You can get in real trouble, too, not like that trouble you get in with mom, where she yells at you and then both of you feel bad. In school, getting in trouble means paper work, a demerit, a note to your folks. Decades later, when you first encounter the employee handbook, you'll already know what "written up" means.

And look, it's not like I hate education. I have a Master's Degree. And I'm not unfamiliar with discipline, either. I went to school with nuns—real, old-fashioned, black habit, white veil nuns. Getting in trouble with a nun was like getting hit by lightning.

I didn't dislike the nuns, either. They hit me a time or two, but I'm not one of these weepy Catholic school veterans. Sister Mary Pius hit you 40 years ago? What did she hit you with, a brick? Quit cryin' and grow up!

But I watch the kids, the little ones, going in that first day and I think, "Kid, this is your first day wearing the saddle."

Then I step down on the gas pedal because I can't be late for work.

✪✪✪

September 19, 2016

Dear Old Times

My mother will be 88 years old on Sunday. I will be 60 next May. My father died 30 years ago. I am an only child. I live near my mother, a two-minute drive. She uses a walker and cannot drive or leave the house alone. She is forgetful. She lives alone.

I spend two hours a day with her, more on my days off. She still fixes her own meals and she remembers to take her medication.

I put out her pills, do her grocery shopping, pick up her prescriptions, clean her house, do her laundry, take her to the doctor, balance her checkbook, pay her bills and change her bed. I have taught myself to wash and set her hair.

I deserve no credit. None at all. I'm her son.

The other day, I went so see her after work, and we were talking about what couples call each other. Honey. Sweetie. Baby. I told her what "bae" means.

My parents married in 1956. They called each other "dear."

"When we got married, everyone we knew, all the couples, called each other 'honey,'" my mother told me. "That's what everybody did.

"So, your father and I talked about it and we decided to call each other, 'dear,' because it was different. We didn't want to be like everyone else."

How hopeful and young do you have to be to have that discussion seriously? How much do you have to believe in the importance of your love that what you call each other has to be discussed, defined, decided on once and for all time?

How involved young people are about every detail of

their love. They leave nothing unexamined because everything is crucial, everything is forever.

It's annoying. It's self-absorbed. It's so beautiful it makes your mouth go dry and your eyes go wet.

A man never knows his mother the way he knows his father. By the time you are 25, you can see your father for what he is, strengths and flaws, and you know if you wan to be like him or you want to be as unlike him as you can.

You never know your mother. She is asexual comfort, the one person who cannot betray you. She uses a walker and forgets things and your heart silently begs her to comfort you, to be the strong one even as she weakens and you have to comfort her.

I know my mother tonight. She was young and it was so important to her what she and her husband would call each other. They wanted it to be different from what other couples called each other, so they had a serious, probably long, discussion and settled on "dear."

I know that young girl. I washed her kitchen floor and took out her trash tonight. I put out her pills. I promised her I'd bring her some toothpaste tomorrow because she is almost out. I call her, "Ma." She and my father called each other "dear."

October 10, 2016

Get Outta My Way, Ya Clown

The other day, a local police department told people to call the cops only if they saw a clown where he didn't belong.

This was in response to nationwide reports of "creepy clown" sightings."

Where doesn't a clown belong?

At a wake? Well, not if the guy in the box is in a clown suit, too. Maybe they worked together.

And what about the birthday party clown who spends a long day pulling handkerchiefs out of his nose and wants to stop on the way home for a beer?

Not long ago, I went out for a beer and I ended up sitting next to a very tall transvestite with visible five o'clock shadow and an Adam's apple the size of a pool ball. She gets to use the bathroom with me, but I'm supposed to call the cops on Mr. Giggles?

So far, the police haven't shot a lot of clowns. You're safer hanging around a graveyard at midnight in a clown suit than you are if you're a black teenager walking down the street with a cellphone in your hand.

Not that there are no risks attached to being a clown suit prankster.

A couple of nights ago, sitting in the newspaper office where I work, I head a scanner call about a clown walking around the parking lot of a suburban mall after closing time.

I don't live in a suburb. I live in a city where something is always on fire and everybody hates everybody else.

"That's it, clown boy," I muttered to myself. "Stay out in the 'burbs. We got people in my neighborhood who'd hit you in the mouth just to see what it feels like to punch a clown."

118

The urban clown needs to watch nose color, too.

The traditional clown nose is red, but you don't want to wear the wrong color nose in the wrong neighborhood. I recommend carrying a blue nose in your pocket, so you can switch from Blood clown to Crip clown without slowing your walk.

If you're in clown gear and you are stopped by the cops, don't pull anything out of your nose. Don't make anything disappear. For God's sake, don't make anything appear. Don't make any balloon animals. In dim light, a balloon animal looks just like an AK-47. You'll get blown out of your big red shoes before you can figure out how to say, "Don't shoot!" in pantomime.

The national psyche is a confusing thing. Here we are, slouching and squabbling toward the end of a historic national election, and everyone's afraid of a creepy clown with orange hair. With any kind of luck, clown season will be over in a few weeks. I hope so. I'm starting to get scared.

December 12, 2016

Oh, Christmas Sweater

I'm a newspaper reporter. I'm 59 years old. I wear a lot of tweed. I swear. I can't count how many house fires, stabbings and shootings I've covered. I'm six feet tall and covered with hair. I smoke, either a pipe or cigars. I drink my whiskey straight and my coffee black. I used to box a little. I'm a fairly good shot. I often refer to the younger reporters as "kid."

In short, I'm nobody's daffodil.

During the Christmas season—and I don't call it "the holiday season"—I'm a big, annoying elf.

I love Christmas like 8-year-old boys love Christmas. During the season, I smoke special Christmas pipe tobacco. On Christmas Eve, I wear a Santa hat to the office. I drive around at night, looking at the lights on the houses. I love Christmas craft fairs and Christmas trees and eggnog. I own a pair of Christmas socks and a couple Christmas ties featuring Santa and elves. The radio in my truck is tuned to the Christmas music station as soon as it's available. I whistle carols.

About three years ago, I decided to buy a Christmas sweater. I wanted something loud, but sincere, and nothing that mocked the holiday.

When, I started my search, I thought what a pity it was that my tiny, immigrant grandmother was dead. Her house was a festival of loud and sincere, including a number of gaudy and cherished Catholic religious articles. As a woman who had no use for irony, she would have been the one to ask.

I did my searching mostly on eBay, the repository of secondhand everything.

I didn't buy anything described as an "ugly Christmas sweater." I wasn't trying to comment on middle-class taste. I was trying to buy a sweater.

If the sweater showed Santa with his pants around his ankles pooping down a chimney, I didn't consider making a purchase. To be blunt, who the hell, having been a child at Christmas, could grow up to buy that sweater?

So, because I love and respect Christmas, it took me three years to find the sweater I wanted.

It's secondhand. I got it on eBay. It's red, long-sleeved. On the front is a big Snoopy with a wreath in his paws. He's smiling. There are holly branches and berries running up both sleeves.

It's American-made, and it was crafted at least 15 years ago, maybe more. I can tell because the design isn't screen-printed onto the sweater. Nope. It's woven right into the wool. As a man who likes to dress well, I can tell you that clothing made overseas is trash compared to what American garment workers used to make.

My wife, who is fashionable, has chosen to regard many of my eccentricities as "cute." I carry a pocket watch. I wear a pinkie ring. She just keeps smiling.

I like the sweater. A lot. I've already worn it to work.

Last week, my wife returned from a mall expedition and told me she'd seen several young men buying loud Christmas sweaters.

"Each one of them had one Christmas sweater, and that's all they bought," she told me. "They must have been going to some kind of ugly Christmas sweater party."

"How old were they?" I asked.

"Early 20s," she said. "Young guys."

My wife works with me. We're both on vacation this week. This morning, she was watching one of those morning talk shows, and the hostess, a birdlike woman in bright blue high heels, was talking about loud Christmas sweaters. She said they're "trending."

"I hit," I told my wife. "Thirty years of tweed and pocket watches and suddenly I'm riding a fashion trend like it's a surfboard."

Take it from an old reporter. Christmas never really goes out of style.

✪✪✪

February 20, 2017

First Date With Russia

America, having spent Valentine's Day 2016 alone, was searching for a soulmate.

America's been talking to Russia online, exchanging emails, keeping things on the down low, and it's been looking pretty good. Russia is manly. Russia is strong. Russia has plans for global expansion. We heard Russia beat up the Crimea, and it made us America hot.

So, America got one of those spray tans, and dyed its hair orange. America put on some Ivanka Trump sleaze heels and a blouse that shows off quite a bit of the Rocky Mountains, and went on a first date with big, strong Russia.

Russia was SO hip. Bought America vodka and caviar. The vodka wasn't cold enough, so Russia had the waiter tortured to death by one of his henchmen.

"OMG!" America squealed. "He has HENCHMEN! Totes adorbs!"

They both told their stories, like you do on first dates.

Russia? The Czar. Stalin. The Gulags. Sooo much snow!

America? Valley Forge. Freedom. Fundamentalist Christianity. The Klan. Evil stepmom Hillary.

"We have a high incarceration rate," America sighed.

"So do we, dahlink," Russia said. "It would be much higher than yours, but we kill a lot of people before they get to jail."

"You're sooo decisive," America said.

"We got creamed in Afghanistan," Russia said.

"So did we!" America said.

We got Muslim terrorists. They got Muslim terrorists. They got people marching through the streets demanding

123

democracy. We got people marching through the streets demanding democracy. They got despised ethnic minorities. We got despised ethnic minorities.

We like vodka. They like vodka. Our poor people are obese. Their poor people are obese. We got meth heads with no teeth. They got drugs that make your skin fall off.

"We're handing our government over to cash-bloated oligarchs," Russia purred.

"Oh, God, show U.S. how to do that," America giggled.

It was getting hot. America could hear the screams of the dying waiter in the basement.

"We tried Britain and France," America sighed. "They're such pansies. Not like you. We hate them now."

"What about NATO?" Russia said. "You're still involved with them, aren't you, my little bowl of borscht?"

"I was sooo drunk when I got in bed with NATO," America said. "I don't even know why I did it. I promise I'll never see them again."

After dinner, it was a blur of clubs, totalitarianism and gypsy music. They danced until dawn.

"In my country, all the buildings are made of concrete," Russia said. "They are gray. They are 50 shades of gray."

"Will you call me?" America said, bosom heaving, mascara smeared with tears of submission.

"First, the election," Russia said.

Finally, after so many years leading the world alone, America has a boyfriend, and he's big and strong and foreign. All the other democratic republics say America is a slut, but they're just jealous. They don't know what love is, not really.

I saw America the other day. She was walking along a beach on the east coast, swaddled in Russian sable, smiling, hair blown by a strong wind from Moscow, a wind that smelled of surrender.

And she pointed towards the sea, pointed at a big gray ship just off the coast.

"That's what my boyfriend drives," she said. "Isn't

it cool?"

It's a wonderful love story, isn't it? I just wish my country wasn't the girl.

✪✪✪

Acknowledgements

✪✪✪

This book would not have been possible without my wife, Deborah Allard Dion, who tells me which of my column ideas are foolish, my mother, Margaret Munroe Dion, to whom I owe my sense of the ridiculous, my father, Eugene Dion, who taught me how tell a story, Rick Newcombe, founder of Creators Syndicate, who found my writing wandering in the desert, Simone Slykhous, an encouraging and talented editor, The Herald News of Fall River, Massachusetts, where I still work and where I learned to write a newspaper column and, always, the people who talk to me in diners and in bars.

About the Author

A veteran reporter and newspaper columnist, Marc Munroe Dion is an old-school newsman who fell out of a Frank Capra movie, complete with pipe and fedora.

Born in the struggling former cotton mill town of Fall River, Massachusetts, Dion spent his childhood moving around the country with his sharp-witted Irish-American mother and his French-Canadian father, both of them chasing the work that left their hometown.

As a teenager in Missouri, Dion dominated his high school debate team and in 1975 was the No. 5 ranked high school orator in America.

The fascination with words continued, as Dion worked his way through college and graduate school as a laborer, bartender and janitor, publishing his first book, a collection of poetry, along the way. He never forgot the people he met at work, or the threadbare, funny stories they told him on loading docks and in bars.

After working for The Associated Press, the Kansas City Star and the Providence Journal as a writer, book reviewer and columnist, he accepted a job on The Herald News, a daily in his hometown of Fall River, where he found more working people with stories to tell and became aware, in his own words, that "the working class is being hunted out of this country like coyotes."

Dion's column, called "Living and Dion," has appeared Mondays in The Herald News for 24 years. During that time, he has won 24 writing awards not only for his column but also for editorial writing and for newspaper stories chronicling the history of Southern New England. He won the New England News Press Association award for Serious Column back to back, in 2010 and 2011.

A loudmouthed independent who still works as a general assignment reporter covering crime, local government and what he calls "the stuff on page 3," Dion says his column is informed, freshened and connected to reality by his daily work as a reporter in a city of 90,000 people.

Tough-minded and unrepentantly working class, Dion's sense of humor sounds more like a barroom than a newsroom, and his political observations are more concerned with issues than political parties.

Dion lives in a 105-year-old three-floor apartment house with his wife, Deborah, who is also a reporter, and two cats.

Land of Trumpin
is also available as an e-book
for Kindle, Amazon Fire, iPad, Nook and
Android e-readers. Visit
creatorspublishing.com to learn more.

o o o

CREATORS PUBLISHING

We publish books.
We find compelling storytellers and
help them craft their narrative,
distributing their novels and collections
worldwide.

o o o

Made in the USA
Monee, IL
26 December 2019

19527886R00081